PUBLISH A NEWSLETTER

From design and editing to production and distribution

Graham Jones

Second Edition

Meeting the final copy deadline

How To Books

By the same author
How to Manage Computers at Work
How to Start a Business from Home

British Library cataloguing-in-publication data
A catalogue record for this book is available from the British Library.

© 1992 and 1995 by Graham Jones

Published by How To Books Ltd, Plymbridge House, Estover Road, Plymouth PL6 7PZ, United Kingdom.
Tel: Plymouth (01752) 735251/695745. Fax: (01752) 695699. Telex: 45635.

First published in 1992
Second edition (revised) 1995

Note: The material contained in this book is set out in good faith for general guidance and no liability can be accepted for loss or expense incurred as a result of relying in particular circumstances on statements made in the book. The laws and regulations are complex and liable to change, and readers should check the current position with the relevant authorities before making personal arrangements.

Typeset by Kestrel Data, Exeter.
Printed and bound in Great Britain by The Cromwell Press, Broughton Gifford, Melksham, Wiltshire.

Contents

List of Illustrations

Preface

to the Second Edition

This is the second edition of this book which has been thoroughly revised to take into account the latest developments in publishing. Since the first edition was published just a couple of years ago, print prices have altered dramatically and computerised publishing has significantly improved. Added to this, newsletter editors now have the worldwide resources of technological innovations such as 'The Internet' at their disposal. These things have all meant that this book needed revising, even though it was originally written very recently. The revisions have brought this book bang up-to-date.

This book is for everyone who wants to produce a newsletter or who is involved in the preparation of a newsletter. Whether you are a member of a club or society, or you are in a large company and want to produce an in-house newsletter for the staff, this book will help.

How to Publish a Newsletter takes you through all of the stages of newsletter production. There is advice on whether you need a newsletter at all, how to plan a newsletter, how to budget your newsletter, how to write it, to edit it and to use illustrations in your pages. There is also information on the various production processes you can use, the legal pitfalls you should avoid and the way to plan for the future. In short, this book is the complete guide to newsletter publishing.

I have aimed the book at relative beginners to publishing. However, that does not mean that more experienced individuals won't find the book useful. The book is structured so that you can choose the part most relevant to your needs. So if you already produce a newsletter but need to know more about using illustrations, you can simply dip into Chapter 6. If you edit a newsletter and want to brush up on your legal knowledge, Chapter 9 is the one for you. No matter what stage of newsletter publishing you are involved in, this book will provide you with some advice and assistance.

Of course, it would be impossible in a book of this size to include absolutely everything there is to know about newsletter publishing. Where I have needed to limit my coverage of a particular area I have provided a clear guide as to where you can get further information. You will find the book sprinkled with references to other books as well as to organisations that can assist. Full contact information is included throughout the book and in 'Further Information' at the back.

I have based the book on my experience in producing newsletters. I run a company which specialises in newsletter editing. This company has produced many newsletters for clients over the last eight years and I have been involved with newsletters for over 20 years altogther. This book is therefore based on sound practical experience and is not just theory. Also, because I was one of the first people to start using computerised publishing systems, back in 1985, I have first hand knowledge of the use of desktop publishing and computers in newsletter production. This book therefore takes into account the best use of computers, but will also help anyone whether or not they use a desktop publishing system.

Finally, I am always interested in newsletters and how they are produced and published. If you have an example you would like to send me then please post it with your details to: ASPECT, PO Box 43, Thatcham, Berkshire RG19 4WH. Perhaps it will get a mention in the next edition of this book.

Graham Jones

1
Why Publish Newsletters?

We are living in the age of information. Never before has so much been written or printed. Never before has there been so much we have needed to read. If you like sailing, for example, there are at least six magazines for you to choose from; if you are a computer-buff you have no less than 35 titles to whet your appetite. Over the last 10 years there has been a staggering 70 per cent rise in the number of general publications available.

Part of the reason for this dramatic increase in reading material has been the increase in our leisure time. We all work less than we did ten years ago, for higher rewards. We have more time to ourselves and more free cash in our pockets. This only explains half the rise in publications, though. A massive number of new publications have come about because of fundamental changes in the technology of publishing.

Ten years ago, if you wanted to produce a publication you would have needed a number of different people with specific skills in writing, editing, design, typesetting and printing. You would also have needed very expensive equipment or you would have been forced to pay the high rates required by typesetting companies. If you had bought the equipment needed to produce your publication you would not have had any change from £250,000 and if you had paid a typesetting company your bill could well have amounted to around £30 per A4 page of setting. Considering these are prices of the early 1980s you can see how expensive publishing was at the time.

Now you can get a page of A4 typeset for less than £1 and the equipment needed to produce your own publication can be bought for less that £2,000. You also no longer need to hire in the skills of a team of individuals. You can do all the work yourself.

This dramatic change in the technology needed to produce a

publication has helped contribute to the rise in the number of titles available. One person with less than £5,000 available to spend can start their own publishing house and produce newspapers, magazines and books. But this technology has also allowed the rapid spread of newsletters: simple, but professional, publications which convey highly specific information or act as a digest of news from a wide range of sources. The newsletter has become a fundamental means of communication in the 1990s, particularly in business.

It would, though, be a mistake to think that newsletters are in any way 'new'. They have not arisen directly from the changes in technology. True, the technological capabilities have meant a massive increase in the number of newsletters being published, but these publications have been around for centuries.

The first recorded 'newsletter' was in fact a newspaper. *The Boston News Letter* was first published in the United States in 1704. Even though this was essentially a newspaper, *The Boston News Letter* was typical of many modern newsletters around today. The publication conveyed commercial information to the growing business population of the colonies. The early settlers in America were traders and up-to-date information on commerce and shipping was vital to their business efforts.

Today, many newsletters provide the same digest of news that cannot easily be obtained by the readers in any other way. These publications act as a convenient way of getting important news in an easy-to-read form. Wouldn't it be far better to get all your important sailing news from a single newsletter, rather than having to wade your way through half a dozen 200-page magazines?

WHAT TYPES OF NEWSLETTERS ARE THERE?

The essential ingredient of all newsletters is that they should convey important information and that this should be short, to the point, easy-to-read, quickly digestible and without waffle. So no matter what you do you can use a newsletter if you need to convey specific information to your audience. Although business has taken hold of the newsletter as an essential part of its communications work, industry and commerce are not the only areas where these publications are effective.

The first newsletter I can remember producing was some 20 years ago when I was a Cadet with the British Red Cross Society.

I helped produce the local detachment's news-sheet of information. Our only technology was a typewriter and a photocopier, but at least we were able to get the important information out to all our members. This was much easier than trying to telephone everyone, or to hope that news given orally at a meeting would somehow filter through to the other members.

This example shows that even without expensive technology it is possible to produce a newsletter that conveys important information no matter what organisation you are in. The Red Cross is a charity which depends entirely on voluntary contributions for its income. We had no budget for the newsletter, but still managed to produce it with help from volunteers. Similarly many charity groups now use the newsletter as a means of communication. My company used to produce the quarterly newsletter for BLISS (Baby Life Support Systems) which helps raise funds for research and treatment of babies born prematurely or with very low birth weight. Using the latest technology this newsletter can be produced professionally without breaking the bank.

The BLISS newsletter contains information of a wide variety. It gives details of branch activities, provides in-depth data on fund raising and gives information on research and development. The audience for the newsletter are members of BLISS, people whose own babies were premature or had problems at birth. Without this newsletter these people would not be able to be up-to-date and would also feel very isolated. The BLISS newsletter helps them keep informed, but also helps the readers feel part of a community, a large extended family of friends.

Charities are not the only groups which can benefit from a newsletter. Churches have always published a parish magazine, but many vicars have found such publications difficult to produce because there is frequently too little contributed to make a magazine worthwhile. With a newsletter format the vicar can write the whole thing and if it only runs to one side of A4 it doesn't matter. More and more churches are producing newsletters, rather than magazines. They can produce more issues a year and so are able to keep the parish church name in front of potential church-goers more frequently.

School newsletters

Schools too benefit from newsletters. The once-a-term magazine, produced by school children themselves, is all very well (I know,

I edited a school magazine when I was seven!) but they are not the best means of conveying information to parents. Traditionally children have taken notes home for mum and dad to let them know half term dates or to provide information on school trips. But children are notorious for forgetting to hand over these slips of paper or for dropping them in puddles when walking home. With newsletters, schools can get the information directly to the parents. This is particularly important since the Education Reform Act 1988 which has allowed schools to be much more aggressive in their 'marketing'. Indeed, schools can now compete for pupils, so they are looking towards newsletters to help convey to parents what a wonderful school they have.

Social interests
If schools can do it, so can you. A family friend travels the world with his family as he is in the Armed Forces. If he had to write back to everyone he knows from across the world his wrist would ache and he would spend half his time writing to us all. Instead, he issues a regular news-roundup which is sent to everyone. We all know how he and his family are getting on and we don't lose touch, which would be easy with someone on the other side of the world.

Club newsletters
What about a newsletter for your club, if you can't think of doing one for your family? No matter what you do in your leisure time there is room for a newsletter. If you are in the local operatic society or are a keen amateur photographer, your group could benefit from a newsletter. You could keep everyone up-to-date with club events, even if some of the members rarely turn up for meetings. A club newsletter can also help strengthen the organisation by making people feel much more as though they belong. You will see later in this book that newsletters are a vital ingredient in helping to produce a feeling of belonging and community, no matter whether it's for the local brass band or for a huge business.

Business newsletters
Of course, as you have already seen, businesses are one of the main providers of newsletters. One of the key areas in which newsletters are employed in business is in passing on information to the staff. Newsletters for employees are big business in themselves, with a

number of firms offering production services for companies who want a staff newsletter. Publications like this are vital in large organisations since they help engender in the employees a feeling of being wanted. In some companies it is all too easy for people on the shop floor to feel isolated from the organisation. With a staff newsletter they are able to feel part of the company. The managers also have a ready-made vehicle for passing on important details to all staff at the same time. Some staff newsletters are so packed with information they are more like newspapers, like *Sweet Talk* from Trebor Bassett or *Agenda* from National Westminster Bank.

Another sector for business newsletters is in communicating with customers. According to business pundits, the coming years are going to see a greater emphasis on customer service. No longer will clients be seen as convenient people to get cash from. Instead, customers will be nurtured, treated as friends and brought in as part of the 'family' that helps the business succeed. Getting customers to feel wanted is becoming a major part of modern business and a newsletter is an ideal method of making clients feel part of the extended 'family'. Many companies issue newsletters to their customers. They also send out newsletters to potential clients so that they think they know the organisation and eventually become part of it by turning themselves into a buying customer.

Newsletters like this are becoming increasingly common. But companies also use newsletters for other more direct means of getting sales. One common area is in marketing support. To help market a product or service companies produce newsletters which show how good the service is, how important the company providing it is, and how effective this combination can be. Europrism is a network of public relations agencies around Europe specialising in healthcare work. Their newsletter, *Healthcare Europe*, is circulated widely throughout Europe and helps show how effective their Europe-wide public relations activities are. In addition, the newsletter provides a digest of information which its readers cannot easily obtain elsewhere. The result is that the potential clients who read it look forward to it so they can get their news. At the same time the publication helps market the PR services of Europrism.

Professional group newsletters

Marketing is a very important part of any business, but it is also

important for other organisations. We have already seen that
schools could usefully employ newsletters to help show how good
they are. Doctors, too, compete for patients and surgeries are now
producing regular newsletters for their patients. These help communicate essential information like surgery times, but are also
used to show how good a particular general practice is at helping
its patients. In this way the surgery is more effectively marketed
and the doctors are able to attract more patients and keep them
longer.

Other professionals are also using newsletters. Lawyers and
accountants are finding that they are a highly effective means of
marketing their services. Binder Hamlyn, for example, publishes
a regular newsletter for businesses in which financial news is
conveyed in a quickly digestible form. The newsletter is sent to
businesses local to a Binder Hamlyn office and this helps generate
calls from potential clients.

Your own newsletter
You could produce a similar newsletter for your kind of business
if you work from home. If you make tea cups out of tree stumps
or offer management consultancy, your home-based business could
do with a newsletter to help drum up sales.

As you can see, virtually anyone can produce a newsletter.
Modern technology has come a long way since *The Boston News
Letter* was started and you no longer need a team of experts to put
together a professional publication. Everything can be done by one
person providing that individual has a real reason to produce the
newsletter.

Key reasons to publish your own newsletter:

● inform
● pass on vital news
● digest news in an easy format
● help establish a 'community'
● keep people interested in your organisation
● act as a marketing aid
● keep staff
● maintain customer confidence
● drum up business
● entertain.

You can probably think of more reasons for your own particular project. But don't forget the two vital ingredients of a newsletter:

1. A newsletter should be a source of information not easily obtainable elsewhere.

2. A newsletter should help its readers feel part of a larger community.

If you think you can achieve these two aims then start your newsletter without delay. You don't need any other reasons to publish a newsletter.

2
Planning Your Newsletter

Even if you have the most wonderful idea for a newsletter, all the equipment to produce it and know exactly who should receive it, you will not get past the first issue without careful planning. This chapter will take you through the planning you need to do, stage by stage. Do not skimp on reading this chapter. Of all the newsletters that are published it is estimated that two out of three fail. All of those failures can be put down to a lack of forward planning. Providing you do the planning properly, your newsletter will succeed and have a long and happy life.

IS YOUR NEWSLETTER NEEDED?

The first stage in your planning exercise is to seriously consider whether your newsletter is actually required or not. People will not read your newsletter if they can get the information elsewhere. They will also not even look at your newsletter if they don't need the information you are supplying. So ask yourself: is the newsletter you are thinking of producing really needed by your potential readers?

To discover this you need to do some research. First of all write down the following things:

- the type or group of people you want to read the newsletter

- the topics each edition will cover

- the frequency you intend producing the newsletter

- the sources of your information.

Having written down your list of information, now gather the following items:

- magazines on the topics you will cover
- books on the topics you will cover
- newsletters on the topics you will cover
- publications received by your target audience
- any competing newsletters.

Now compare your two piles of information. You should have one set of notes which shows what you want to provide. You should also have an assortment of literature which reveals what is already available to your target audience. By comparing the two, you will be able to see whether there is a gap for your idea; and by looking closely at competing newsletters you will be able to see if there is any area which they do not cover. If this falls neatly into the field in which you want to publish, then the chances are your newsletter could succeed.

Don't do this research in a hurry. Take your time. Construct your lists of what you want in the newsletter over a period of days; collect the literature you need over a period of weeks. Only then will you be able to make an honest assessment of the likely chances of your newsletter succeeding. If your potential audience already receives the information you want to provide, it's likely there is no need for your idea. But don't give up. Your research efforts will reveal a gap in the information and you will be able to re-define your ideas to fit that gap.

Naturally, if you are a member of a club or association which does not have a newsletter, or if your customers do not receive regular information from you, the research is easier. You should do this research all the same, however, as you will be able to pinpoint topics which need covering because they are not well represented in other literature your fellow members or customers might receive.

This essential research is not the only preparatory work you must do, though. Simply locating a gap in the available information and getting on with your newsletter could be unproductive. You need to check with potential readers whether they would like such a publication. This is basic **market research**, but unless you do it, your newsletter is doomed to fail. So check with your fellow club members if they would like a newsletter; ask your customers whether they would like to know more about your company; and seek the thoughts of your staff if you are proposing an **in-house newsletter**. If your newsletter is likely to meet a gap in their information you should receive a vote of confidence, but if your initial research has been incomplete, talking to your potential readers will reveal the likely problems you could encounter. If you intend publishing a newsletter on a commercial basis, selling subscriptions, then this market research is vital. If you do not find out exactly what your potential purchasers require, you will flounder after the first issue.

If after some simple market research and your analysis of the potential gap for your publication you discover that you were right, that your newsletter is needed, then you can go on to plan it properly. If, however, your preparatory work showed that there is no place for your newsletter, do not worry. Your basic research should have revealed what gaps exist and what your potential readership wants. You can then use this information to develop your ideas further.

UNDERSTANDING NEWSLETTER PSYCHOLOGY

Having found your gap for a newsletter, you now need to become something of an amateur psychologist to carry on with your planning. The most important part of the brain you will need to understand as a publisher is the emotional part. Although your market research will have revealed gaps in factual areas which need covering, what you are going to have to provide to win readers and keep them is **emotional stimulation**.

So you don't believe me? You think that newsletter readers are merely seeking information they can't easily get elsewhere, that newsletters are not seen as a means of stimulating our emotions. You may think this is too weird an idea to consider at the outset of your planning for a new newsletter. To see what I mean, let's look at our first case study.

Case study: The estate agent

Tony Smythe runs the only estate agency in Westfield. He employs two assistants and a secretary. Because Westfield is a tightly knit community he enjoys the bulk of all house sales in the area, but he is in constant threat of business being taken over by the bigger and cheaper agents in the nearby large town of Goldmead.

Tony comes up with the bright idea of a local newsletter for Westfield. His idea is that the newsletter should contain community information that is not covered by the local newspaper which is published in Goldmead and only pays scant attention to the news from Westfield. By being a local newsletter the Smythe publication will help focus on the community. At the same time, the newsletter could contain information on houses, planning proposals in the area and so engender loyalty from the people in the area. Tony hoped that by engaging local support in this way he could maintain his current leading position and keep the preying vultures from Goldmead at arms' length. Tony checked his idea out with a few friends who live in the town and also discussed it with the regulars at the Bat and Ball pub. He was sure he was right and that the newsletter would succeed.

Tony's secretary was given the job of putting the information together. Tony and his assistants collected all the details and at the end of the month Alison, his secretary, was asked to put together the two-page newsletter. It took her a while to work out the multiple column features of her word processor, but she managed it and was able to make everything almost fit two pages. The last article had to be crammed in a bit, but at least it was all there. Tony was pleased anyway, and he asked her to run off 300 copies so that he could deliver one to every house and have a few left over for the office and the pub.

Unfortunately, Tony hadn't realised how long it would take to deliver the copies. So he gave up after the first 100 and got his assistants to deliver the rest later in the week. When he went to the pub on Friday night he was a bit shocked at the reaction. Half the regulars hadn't even seen the newsletter and those who did see it said they hadn't realised it was his publication. Everyone he spoke to had thrown it away.

Never mind, Tony thought, it was the first issue and people would get used to it. Once they knew it was his newsletter they would all support him.

The second issue took a bit longer to prepare. Tony had a couple of meetings with a local property developer which had taken up much of the time he had set aside to write the material. Then when he did have time to write it Alison had got a couple of days holiday, so it was a week later before she could type it up. Then Tony's assistants were busy at a new housing development in the evenings so it was another week before the deliveries were made. Never mind, Tony thought again, it was only a fortnight later than he'd hoped. He was sure no-one would notice.

He hadn't expected the reaction he received at the pub on Friday night. He thought everyone would have seen it this time—after all, he'd been in the pub a few weeks ago and told them all about the newsletter, so now they'd be geared up to expecting it. But the regulars hadn't seen the newsletter, or if they had they couldn't remember it. The main reason, said the locals, was that since the second edition hadn't come out a month after the first, they'd all thought Tony had scrapped the idea.

Tony did scrap the idea after that. He thought it wasn't worth all the effort. He'd gone to a great deal of trouble, even asking the people in the area if they would like his newsletter. And even though they had been very positive about his idea, not one of the people he had spoken to had actually read his newsletter. They had all ended up in the waste paper bin. What an ungrateful bunch of people live in this area, thought Tony.

The lessons learned
What can be learned from this scenario? Although Tony's idea was right, that there was a gap for his proposed newsletter, his plans were scuppered because he failed to take into account the psychology of his audience and look at how he could stimulate their emotions. Had he made these people excited or happy with his newsletter the reaction would have been altogether different. His mates down the pub would have said 'jolly good newsletter' and 'brilliant stuff, can't wait until the next issue'. Instead the reaction was cold and negative. He had not stimulated his audience.

Another problem with the psychological planning of Tony's newsletter was the fact that it was not what his readers had expected. Clearly, from his descriptions of what he was planning, the readers were thinking they were going to get something different. As a result many of them did not even realise that the newsletter which fell onto their doormat was Tony's. He had failed to meet their psychological expectations, which were for something different. The psychology of publications is a very involved topic. The lessons to be learned from Tony's experience are:

• your newsletter must match the expectations of your audience

• you must stimulate the emotions of your readers.

PSYCHOLOGICAL PLANNING

The reaction to your newsletter will depend on three features:

- the **'look and feel'** of the newsletter
- the **frequency** of publication
- and the **methods used** to produce the newsletter.

To help you make sure that you are preparing the right kind of newsletter for your readers, you need to complete the following questionnaire. By analysing your answers you will begin to see the sort of publication that will best suit your potential readers.

1. What is the average age of your main target reader?

2. What sex are most of your readers?

3. What work do your readers do?

4. What is the average salary of your readers?

5. What is the marital status of your average reader?

6. How many children does your average reader have?

7. What type of house does your average reader live in? Is it a flat, a semi-detached, a detached, a mansion?

8. Does your average reader own or rent their house?

9. What educational standard does your average reader have?

10. What newspaper does your average reader take each day?

11. What sort of magazines does your average reader look at?

12. What sort of professional publications do your readers see?

13. Where will your readers be most likely to read the newsletter: in the bath, on the train, in front of the TV, in bed, where?

14. What time of day will the newsletter be seen?

15. Are your average readers in good health with no major physical problems?

These questions are fundamental to helping you build a psychological profile of your readers. If you do not take time to get the answers right you will produce a newsletter which does not match the expectations of your audience. You will therefore alienate them as the newsletter gives the wrong psychological impact. That's when they throw away your newsletter. To see how the answers of these questions would help, let's first look at the estate agency case.

Case history: The estate agent
If Tony Smythe had completed his **psychological profiling** of his average audience he would have come up with the following answers:

1. Age: 40

2. Sex: 75 per cent male

3. Work: City executives

4. Salary: Over £40,000

5. Marital status: Married

6. Children: Three

7. House: Five-bed detached

8. House status: Owned

9. Education: University

10. Newspaper: *The Times/Financial Times*

11. Magazines: *Country Life, Good Housekeeping, Yachting Monthly*

12. Professional publications: *Money Marketing*

13. Place read: In front of TV

14. Time read: Mid-evening

15. Health status: Good

From this information Tony could have realised that his potential audience would mostly be busy men who would be looking at the newsletter when they were tired after a hard day's work and distracted by children and the TV. These men would also be used to reading top class publications including some excellent glossies. They would be intelligent and generally up-market, and they would therefore be likely to be put off by anything which seems less than high standard.

The lessons learned
Looking at this psychological information about Tony Smythe's potential readers, we can see where he went wrong. The publication he provided did not match their expectations; they were thinking of a much more professional looking newsletter than an untrained secretary could produce. Indeed, Alison herself admitted that the second page of the first issue was tatty because she had to cram in the last article to make it fit. The result was that the potential readers were offended and threw it away. Their only emotion which had been triggered was one of disgust. Had Tony done his psychological profiling he would have realised what his readers wanted and would therefore have been able to meet their expectations. Having done that he could have set about triggering their emotions.

EMOTIONAL TARGETS

Providing you get the newsletter right, you still need to get the emotions of the readers going. You will want to provide a newsletter that triggers the following emotional reactions at some stage:

● agreement
● happiness

- sadness
- anger
- shock
- horror
- fright
- amazement
- laughter
- sexual arousal
- pleasure
- empathy
- sympathy

If, like Tony, you do not psychologically profile your potential readers you will not know which emotions you should trigger most frequently. The 40-year old males who could read Tony's newsletter are successful and generally well-off. They would look to a publication to provide them with material that made them happy, amazed them and even aroused their sexual feelings! A publication which triggered these emotions and met their overall expectations would be bound to succeed, but Tony's newsletter made the readers angry at its amateurishness. He had triggered the wrong emotions for his audience and so lost their attention.

Test yourself
To see whether you think all this is hogwash, try the following test. Complete the psychological profile questionnaire on page 23 but this time give the answers which directly relate to yourself. Then write down a summary of your answers in the same way as was shown for Tony Smythe's estate agency.

Now list the emotional triggers which would be likely to apply to someone who fits this psychological profile. Use any of the terms listed on pages 25–26. Now take a look at yesterday's newspaper and mark the stories you read with interest. You should see that each of the stories you have marked triggers one of the emotions you have selected as being targets for your psychological profile.

Using emotions in planning
Now that you have seen how important emotion is in producing your newsletter you will be able to start planning properly. You should have already produced a psychological profile of your average reader and should have a list of the emotions you want to

trigger most frequently. Now you can begin to develop a newsletter that will meet the psychological expectations of the people you want as readers and know that you will be able to keep them interested provided you keep hooking their favourite emotions.

Case study: The student union

Millchester is a large, sprawling new town in the South. It has a modern university campus, built in the last ten years. There are some 4,000 students who mostly live on site. Their social life extends around the student union, which produces a student newspaper with help from the local paper once every two weeks. However the executives of the union want to get information out more quickly and have come up with the idea of producing their own newsletter to fill the gap between the newspapers coming out. The local paper cannot commit any more help and finances won't run to a weekly newspaper, so the newsletter seems like the ideal solution to the difficulties of keeping students informed more regularly.

Steve Wilson is the student executive in charge of publicity. It has fallen to him to produce the newsletter. His first task is to find out if students want the newsletter. He asks around the union building and many students think it is a good idea. He also mentions the idea at the weekly student union assembly where it receives support too. So the basic idea seems acceptable.

Steve then decides to complete a psychological profile of the target readers. Although he knows a great deal about students, committing this profile to paper helps him formulate the plans for the newsletter more solidly. His profile of average potential readers reads as follows:

1. Age   19

2. Sex   60% male 40% female

3. Work   Studying

4. Salary   Grants up to £2,500

5. Marital status   Single

6. Children   None

7. House	Campus bedsit
8. House status	Rented
9. Education	University
10. Newspaper	*The Guardian/Daily Mail*
11. Magazines	*Viz, Private Eye, Marie Claire, Economist, Men Only, Playgirl*
12. Professional publications	Various technical journals
13. Place read	In bedsit
14. Time read	At breakfast
15. Health status	Good

From this information Steve knows that his potential readers are not likely to be distracted while reading, but don't want information that is likely to make them spend a great amount of cash because they don't have much money. The newsletter would need to be entertaining and stimulating, to make it a good start to the day. So the emotions which need triggering are: laughter, amazement, happiness, sexual arousal and pleasure.

We also know that the students are generally in good health, so they won't need special equipment to help them read, or a large typesize because of poor eyesight. You see how the answers to these questions can so easily change the way you plan your newsletter; if you provided a tightly typed newsletter to people with reading difficulties you would not win their support so easily. If your readers are handicapped in any way you would not gain their psychological positive reaction if you produce a complex, three-fold newsletter that is difficult for anyone with less than 100 per cent manual dexterity to handle. These may seem basic parts of your plan, but such things are forgotten by many newsletter producers and are responsible for many failures.

So with a good profile like Steve's you can get on with the next stage of your plan for your newsletter—'look and feel'.

LOOK AND FEEL

Now that you know what your readers expect, and what emotions you are going to have to stimulate, you can work out what you want your newsletter to look like and what sort of 'feel' you want to give it. You will have to consider a number of different items to get the right look and feel for your newsletter. These are:

- page size
- number of pages
- paper quality
- paper weight
- use of colours
- overall design

The most important consideration in all this is physical size.

Deciding the page size
Your newsletter can be any size you want. It can be:

- A5 (210 x 148 mm)
- A4 (297 x 210 mm)
- A3 (420 x 297 mm)
- American letter
- Americal legal
- British legal
- any other 'bastard' size (printers refer to non-standard sizes as 'bastards').

The size you choose is important as it gives immediate impact. If your readers are busy people and will read the newsletter on the train to work, you will not win their support and friendship if you produce an A3 publication that is difficult to hold open in a packed commuter carriage. Choose the size of your publication with care so that it matches what your readers expect and also wins their subconscious support.

Deciding the number of pages
The next important factor in the look and feel stakes is the number of pages you produce. Newsletters can be anything from one side of paper to hundreds of pages. What you produce will depend upon

a variety of factors, but do not provide your readers with one page if they expect 24. Similarly, if you are providing a newsletter for people to read on a short commuter journey, they will not give you their support if you provide more than a couple of pages. The maximum number of pages you produce should not be determined by how much you think you can write. Instead, limit yourself to a number of pages determined by the details extracted from your psychological profile. If your newsletter is for your club and most of the members are busy young mums, they will not want a 48-page newsletter to wade through every month, no matter how interesting the words are.

When choosing the number of pages limit yourself to the following choices:

1	8	24	64	128
2	12	36	80	
4	16	48	96	

The reason for these figures is that they represent the most commonly used lengths for publications. They are therefore familiar lengths to readers, thus helping them feel comfortable with your publication. If you produce a seven-page newsletter, for example, your readers can feel a bit cheated and may even look for the extra page which they wrongly think is missing. Again you score negative subconscious points and begin to lose the support of your readers in this way.

Another reason for these page lengths is that they will be the most economical to produce.

Choosing the right paper
The paper your newsletter is printed on also has a significant psychological effect. If your audience is expecting something to match their high standards you will not be forgiven if you print your newsletter on low quality paper. Similarly, if your audience is likely to view the newsletter as an instant information source which is thrown away within minutes of reading it, you will be viewed suspiciously if you print on glossy, art type paper.

Paper types
You should choose from the following basic paper types:

- newsprint
- bond
- matt
- silk
- art

Newsprint is the lowest quality and art is the highest. If you are environmentally conscious you can get all these types of paper made from recycled materials. Your printing firm will be able to help but specialist suppliers of paper advertise in *Creative Review*, a monthly magazine which is available from most large newsagents.

Paper weight

Another factor in paper choice is the weight or thickness of the paper. To confuse everyone paper is weighed by the square metre, though you cannot buy a single sheet of paper at that size! All paper weights are measured in 'gsm', which represents grams per square metre. The higher the weight, the thicker the paper. Photocopying paper, for example, is around 80 gsm. The paper of this book is about 90 gsm and the cover of this book is 240 gsm.

If you choose a weight of paper which does not match the expectations of your audience, you will not win readers. For example, say you are producing an in-house newsletter for the staff of your company. If you produce the newsletter on thick, glossy paper, the staff will automatically assume that the newsletter has a big budget. This will not go down well when what they really want is more car parking spaces. Why can't money be spent on improving the car park instead of a glossy newsletter, they will ask. In fact, as you will see later, the difference in price between matt paper and glossy paper is quite small; but the difference in psychological impact is immense. You should be aware of this.

Using colour printing

The next most important psychological consideration in your newsletter is colour. There's not enough space to deal with this subject in detail here; indeed, psychologists have written tomes on the theme of colour psychology. It is a complex subject, but you need to consider some basics if you are to get your newsletter right from the start.

Why have colours?

Simple: we see in colour. We are not like cats who only see in black and white. We like colours, we expect colours. Colour makes things seem alive, vibrant and attractive. Something which is merely black and white appears harsh, cold and formal. Although you will need to be acutely aware of the expectations of your audience, you should seriously consider adding colour to your newsletters. This does not mean you should fill the pages with glossy colour pictures. You can add a single colour to black and splash it around for boxes, headings, tinted backgrounds and so on. An additional colour adds little to the printing cost of your newsletter so it is well worth considering.

What colours should I choose?

Printers tend to use two colours widely; these are known as 'process blue' and 'process red', but you can have any colour you like. Consider the emotional impact of colours: blue appears to be cold and unfriendly; red has overtones of danger and calling for attention; greens are seen as open, inviting and relaxing; purples are associated with formality and correctness; pink is seen as friendly and soft; yellow is seen as calm.

As you can see, the choice of the colour you want to use is dependent upon the psychological expectations of your audience and the impact you wish to achieve. Take a look at other publications and you will become instantly aware of the strong presence of red. This colour calls for attention and makes people notice its presence. The cover of this book is red, for instance. If in any doubt about colours, choose red.

Overall design

The final aspect of the look and feel of your newsletter is the overall design it will have. The most noticeable thing about any design is the number of columns. The second important feature is the typeface you choose. Finally, the use of pictures has to be considered.

Columns

Your newsletter can have a single column, or as many columns as you can comfortably fit on the size of paper you are using. The simple rule to remember is that if you have few columns the newsletter will look formal, intelligent, almost academic. If you have a large number of columns it will look informal, down-market and newsy. The choice is yours depending on the expectations of your audience and the psychological impact you are trying to create. If, like many people, you are producing a newsletter on A4 paper you will find that three columns is an excellent compromise if you are in any doubt.

Choosing typefaces

There are thousands of typefaces available. Even if you are only going to use an ordinary typewriter for your newsletter, you will still have a choice of the way the type is presented.

There are two basic sorts of typeface, though professional typographers have five categories. The two sorts you need to consider are:

- serif faces
- sans serif faces.

A serif typeface is the kind you are reading now. The characters have little curls at the edges. A sans serif typeface is the kind without any curls, as used for the page headings in this book.

There has been a great deal of research on how we read and what influences our abilities. That research has shown that for long pieces of text serif typefaces are easier for us to read. Sans serif typefaces are not suitable for long pieces of text as they reduce the speed with which we can read. However, sans serif typefaces do have impact and clarity. These are the reasons for many publications using serif typefaces for their main text, but sans serif typefaces for headings.

Although this is the basic choice made by many publishers, you should make your final consideration based upon your analysis of your potential readers. Mostly you will make the standard choices. Even so, there are thousands of typefaces to choose from.

Look at a range of typefaces in books and magazines. You will see that some appear to be formal and academic, others look open, inviting and less formal. If your newsletter is to be academic, perhaps will only have one column and is for top scientists, you will reduce your impact if you choose a modern looking typeface that is open and informal. Likewise, if you are producing an up-beat publication for your youth club, you won't get many readers if you use an academic looking typeface.

The final selection of your typeface will of course depend on the technology you are using to produce your newsletter, but you need to make some basic decisions at this stage as to the sort of typeface you want to use.

Pictures

The final part of the look and feel you need to consider are pictures. Again, whether or not you include pictures, and the type of illustrations you use, will depend very much on the psychological profile of your readers which you have drawn up. If, for instance, your readers are producing a student union newspaper, the readers will not expect high quality illustrations from top photographers and artists. Cartoons and silly photos will be more their line. But you probably would not get away with cartoons in a serious academic newsletter for scientists, who would expect factual illustrations of experiments. Choose the sort of picture you need to match the psychological profile of your readers.

Should you have pictures?
Yes. Even if you can't think of exactly what pictures you would include at this stage, consider the type of picture you would like to use. Anything from a diagram to a full colour photo, but think of pictures. Readability research has shown conclusively that when pictures are included, people understand what they are reading more easily, they remember it more readily and they enjoy it more completely. No matter what the psychological profile of your readers, the newsletter you plan to produce will benefit from illustrations.

LOOK AND FEEL PLAN

Having considered the various options, you are now ready to complete your outline plan for your newsletter. By filling in the following table you will be able to draw up a basic picture of your newsletter. This information will also be vital if you wish to get your newsletter printed by a professional printing company. It is worth getting this outline done now, so that when you come to print your newsletter you will be well prepared.

● reader profile
● physical size of newsletter

- number of pages
- quality of paper
- weight of paper
- colours to be used
- number of columns
- style of typeface
- picture categories.

FREQUENCY

Another important factor in the psychological reaction to your newsletter is how frequently you publish it. If your readers are busy people who want information that is useful, but not vital, they will not appreciate a daily newsletter. Similarly, if your readers depend upon your publication for up-to-the-minute information on their jobs they will not support your quarterly newsletter.

The frequency with which you produce your newsletter will depend upon the information you convey and the expectations of your audience. Newsletters can be hourly (yes, there are some) or annual. Many are monthly and quite a few are quarterly. All too frequently, though, people consider the frequency of publication according to their budget. You should always consider the frequency of publication according to the expectations and requirements of your audience.

PRODUCTION

You now know roughly what your newsletter will look like and when it will come out. You have a more complete idea of its readers and how they will view the newsletter. You also have a clue as to its physical appearance. The next stage in planning is to think about the production of your newsletter. You will need to consider the following aspects of production in your initial planning for your newsletter:

- information sources
- writing
- editing
- design
- printing
- distribution

Information sources

These will be considered in more detail in Chapter 4. For now you simply need to think about where you will get the information from. Will the likely sources have costs attached to them? How easy will it be to get the information when you need it? Will the information come in a usable form, or will it need working on? These are essential questions in your planning. If you cannot provide satisfactory answers your newsletter may be a non-starter. You could have the best idea for a newsletter ever thought up, but if you cannot get the information to put in it you are doomed.

Writing

Who will write your newsletter? How much time will it take? What equipment will be needed? When will the writers be available to do the writing? When can writing not be done?

You must answer these questions to be sure you have worked out the implications of producing your newsletter. If you haven't got the time or expertise to do the writing, you will need assistance. This will have cost implications and so it needs careful consideration at the outset.

Editing

Having got the words, who is going to edit the newsletter? Editing is not just a simple matter of making everything fit into the space allocated; it is deciding what to include, what to leave out, the order in which material is presented, who will write the articles you want and how they should be written. Editing is about ensuring that the newsletter continually meets the expectations of the audience. If you are unable to take on the task or do not have the time, you must find someone who can do the work. This will have cost implications and will also have time restrictions. The editor you choose may not be able to work according to your timetable, for instance.

Design

Many editors are capable publication designers, others are not. Can you design your newsletter, making each issue look attractive? Can you ensure that every issue looks different, yet still retains the consistent look and feel of previous issues? This sort of work requires expertise and skill. If you do not have those skills you will need to employ extra assistance. Once again there are cost and time implications which will need analysis at this planning stage.

Printing

The method of printing you choose should match the expectations of your reader profile. If you are producing a quick and ready newsletter, photocopying may be sufficient, but if your readers are going to expect a high quality item, you will need proper printing. Again these considerations need to be made now so that you can properly cost your newsletter.

Printing choices

There are several choices available to you for your newsletter. You can choose any of the following:

- stencil duplicating
- photocopying
- laser colour photocopying
- laser printing
- high street copy shop printing
- offset lithographic printing
- letterpress printing
- gravure printing.

Stencil duplicating is the cheapest form of printing since you do all the work yourself. **Gravure printing** is the most expensive since it is not widely available and is a specialist process. I have separated out **high street copy shops** from general **offset litho printers**. (Offset litho is the standard form of printing used by commercial printing companies). The reason for this is that the technology used by many copy shops for printing is of a lower quality than that used by larger commercial printing companies. Beware, though, as you will see later you can be charged considerably more for the high street service.

At this stage all you need to be concerned about is the method of printing which your psychological profile requires. In most instances you will choose either photocopying, laser printing or offset litho printing.

We will come to distribution later on in the book.

PRODUCTION PLAN

Now that you have considered the ways in which your newsletter will be put together, you can complete the following table to produce your own production plan. With this information in writing you will be able to move on to the next important stage of planning: finances. Ask yourself:

● Where will the information for the newsletter come from? How much is the information likely to cost?

● Who will write the newsletter? What are the likely costs?

● Who will edit the newsletter? What are the likely costs?

● Who will design the newsletter? What are the likely costs?

● What type of printing is required? What are the likely costs?

Now you can take your four vital plans—the psychological profile, the look and feel plan, the frequency outline and the production plan—to the next stage of setting up your newsletter, the financial planning.

'It's actually arrived on time!'

3
Financing Your Newsletter

CONTROLLING THE COSTS

It doesn't matter whether you are producing your newsletter for a group of friends or you are the head of a publications department in a multi-national conglomerate, your newsletter will cost something. If your newsletter is to succeed you must prepare detailed and accurate budgets. If you do not cost out your newsletter properly it will certainly fail. Either you will be unable to meet the demands of your plans, or you will not be able to continue publishing because you are spending money but not producing any income.

There are two stages to your financial plans: the costs of producing your newsletter; the income the newsletter can generate.

The costs of producing your newsletter will fall into the following areas:

- information gathering
- writing
- editing
- design
- typesetting
- printing
- distribution
- promotion.

You must first work out the costs involved in producing the newsletter geared specifically to the profile of your readers, which you discovered in the exercises in Chapter 2. You will need your plans from Chapter 2 at your side in order to work out the costs involved. If the costs for producing your 'ideal' newsletter are higher than you expected, do not be despondent. Later on in this chapter you will find ways of offsetting the costs, even making a profit. Don't forget, there is no such thing as 'it can't be done'. Everything is always possible, so your ideal newsletter is feasible, no matter what figures you arrive at during the following costing exercise. Also, in the sections that follow you will find plenty of hints on how to minimise costs without sacrificing your ideals.

INFORMATION GATHERING

You should by now have a good idea of the sort of information you wish to publish and the material your potential readers expect. Now you have to look in detail at where you will get that information. The sources open to you are:

- other publications
- personal contacts
- public relations agencies
- press releases
- press conferences
- on-line computer databases, or the 'Internet'
- television
- radio
- interviews
- anonymous tip-offs.

Each of these information sources has cost implications which you will need to assess.

Using other publications

These can be anything from other newsletters to newspapers, magazines, books or encyclopaedias. However you will need to subscribe to the publications you need. Your newsletter will not be well-informed if you rely upon using the occasional copy of a useful magazine you happen to see. Complete the following table to work out the costs of your publication sources.

Table 1

Type of publication	Title	Price/year	Frequency
Newsletters			
Newspapers			
Magazines			
Books			
Total price			

You now know how much money these sources of information will cost. Keep this table handy, you will need it later.

Free publications
Do not neglect free publications. These can be a very useful source of material for your newsletter. Keep your eye out for free publications which apply to the subject matter of your newsletter, then ensure that your name goes on the mailing list. Also, by getting your name on the free publications' mailing lists, you are likely to be targeted by other suppliers of information with direct mailshots. The information contained in these will be freely sent to you and it could be useful in your newsletter.

Using personal contacts
Information from people you know will form a great part of the content of your newsletter. But don't go thinking that this will not cost you anything!

If you are producing a staff newsletter, for example, you may think it appropriate to pay a small fee for information provided. Even if you don't pay the staff themselves it may be appropriate to pay money into the company's 'widows and orphans' fund, or some such scheme, to show that you appreciate the information. If you do not pay your contributors, or show them that you value the information, your sources will quickly dry up.

Likewise, if you are producing a local newsletter for your area housing association, you will need to cough up for the information. You may not need to pay the providers directly, but you will need to buy them a drink at the local pub, or even invite them round for dinner every once in a while. In either event, you will need some cash.

To work out how much you need to spend on personal contact sources complete the following table:

Table 2

Person	No of contacts/year	Annual entertainment cost

Using public relations agencies
PR companies will be very keen to supply you with information. They hope that all the 'free' material they give you will end up in your pages, so providing publicity for their clients. Once you set up a newsletter you can expect constant attention from PR companies. This is not a blessing, in spite of the so-called free material.

Public relations agencies can be pests. They will frequently provide you with totally irrelevant material which is of no interest. Then they will call you and ask you why you didn't use the material. You will reply that your newsletter on budgerigars has no need for the latest information on computer controlled washing machines, thank you very much. The PR company will reply, ah yes, but have you considered how useful it would be to someone to have a computer controlled washing machine so they could spend more time with their budgie.

This scenario is not a joke. It is real. Professional PR people believe that writers make these sort of things up. We do not, they happen every day. For example, I received a press release announcing a new device for a mainframe computer. I then got a telephone call from the PR company asking me if I got the information and would I like to go to a press conference on the topic. I was asked these questions in two other telephone calls from other people at the PR company. Did I mind? Yes. I have never written anything about mainframe computers and I do not edit any publications that include details of such machines. The result of the PR company's lack of professionalism was my time being wasted, and time is always money. And that was just one instance. On average in a year I estimate that ineffective public relations companies actually cost me £1,500 in lost productive time. If you will be using PR agencies as a source of information you will need to budget for the loss in production time. You will also need to consider entertainment expenses for PR consultants as you will need to buy them drinks and meals every now and again in order to ensure you remain on their mailing list.

Try completing the following table to work out the costs of using PR agencies as sources of material.

Table 3

PR Agency	No of contacts/year	Time costs	Entertainment

There is always a bright side to each potential problem, though. Your PR company contacts will every now and then give you usable information for your newsletter. They will also provide you with plenty of useless press releases; you will be able to use the back of these for scrap paper, thus reducing your stationery bill!

Using press releases

Most of the press releases you receive will come from PR agencies. Nine out of every ten will be unusable and will simply be thrown away. Indeed, you won't even look at many of them; once you see the headed notepaper you immediately switch off and chuck the gumph in the bin. I don't even bother to open the envelopes if I recognise the franking mark. There could be an offer hard to resist inside, but when you receive a large volume of press releases you will be prepared to take the risk in order to reduce the effort required to wade through them.

In most instances you will not be able to use the good press releases verbatim. The vast majority are badly written, leave out vital facts and are not geared to the psychological requirements of your readers. So don't think that you can rely on press releases to provide you with free copy; they are useful for information only.

To get press releases you will need to be on some essential mailing lists. These are:

PNA
13-19 Curtain Road
London EC2A 3LT
Tel: 0171-377 2521

PIMS
4 St John's Place
London EC1M 4AH
Tel: 0171-250 0870

Editors/PR Newslink
9-10 Great Sutton Street
London EC1V 0BX
Tel: 0171-251 9000

You should also write to public relations agencies which deal with your particular topics and ask to be kept informed and to be put on the press release mailing list. To find out which PR agencies do what kind of things you need:

The Hollis Directory
Contact House
Lower Hampton Road
Sunbury on Thames
Middlesex TW16 5HG
Tel: 01932 784781

When it comes to budgeting for using press releases you will need to cost for buying *Hollis* each year (£79.50) and for time needed to rewrite the press releases to suit your audience. To budget for the time you need to take to do this you can only provide an estimate, but at least it will help you sort out your finances. To work out the estimate do the following calculation:

No of pages x No of press release/pages x 15

This will give you the approximate cost in whole pounds of

converting press releases into copy for your readers. Enter the total figure in the table below.

Table 4

Cost of using press releases	£
Subscription to Hollis Directory	£
Total press release costs	£

Attending press conferences

When something very important has to be announced there will be a press conference. Sadly the PR industry's definition of importance is not the same as most editors'. The result is a large number of press conferences which waste the time of writers. Fewer and fewer people seem to be attending press conferences these days, unless the story is of major national importance. You should only consider going to press conferences if you are sure the story is vital to the success of your newsletter. Otherwise they will be a drain on your time and resources.

The costs of press conferences include:

- time taken for travelling
- time for attendance
- travelling costs.

The vast majority of press conferences are held in London, Manchester or Edinburgh. Naturally, every locality has press conferences but these are usually only for local issues. If you are not within an hour of a major centre, forget press conferences. They will simply waste your time and help kill off your newsletter. Far better to pick up the news when it is published elsewhere. Also, if you can't go to a press conference, the PR company will always supply you with the information given out to those who did attend.

If you think press conferences will be important sources of information, try doing the following calculation:

A = Distance to press conference centre x 2 x 0.5

B = Time taken to press conference centre in hours x 2 + 1

C = B x 30

D = A + C

D is your total cost for attending a press conference, taking into account travelling costs and time missing from active newsletter production. Now you need to multiply D by the number of press conferences you expect to attend each year. In general, you should not really attend more press conferences than the number of issues you will produce in a year. So if you are a monthly newsletter, expect to attend an average of 12 press conferences, if they are going to be important sources. If not, keep away!

Fill in the following table to help in your cost calculations:

Table 5

Cost of attending press conferences:	£
(D x No of press conferences/year)	

To help get invited to important press conferences you should be sure to be on all the mailing lists for press releases. You should also be in touch with any professional organisations which have interests in the area of your newsletter. You should also subscribe to the *UK Press Gazette*, which includes a diary of events for each week, including many press conferences.

One other tip: get yourself on the mailing list of the free quarterly journal, the *Journalists' Handbook*. This contains a large number of information contact points and includes plenty of diary dates, such as press conferences.

Using on-line computer databases

There is a vast array of material available on **computer data-bases**. If you have a computer you can access these databases no matter where they are in the world. You can extract the information you want, save it on your computer and then use the data for your newsletter. The costs for getting this information are the price of your telephone calls and the fees the owners of the databases charge you to access their computer records. Here is a brief rundown of the popular database systems, with particular emphasis on their costs. More information on the databases mentioned can be found in Chapter 4.

Profile
For many newsletters Profile will be a very useful database. This is owned by the *Financial Times* and includes a whole host of information. It provides the text of most national newspapers for the last five years or so. You can also get the text of magazines like *New Scientist* or *Marketing Week*. There is the text of foreign sources, like the Asahi News Service, an important Japanese daily news information network, and *The Washington Post*. Added to this is data from many other specific information sources.

Like other databases you simply search for information that interests you. The database comes back very quickly to let you know if it has the information and if so, how much of it and what kind it is. Say, for example, you were putting together a newsletter for your local residents association, and that in each issue you wanted to highlight what other similar associations had been doing up and down the country. Rather than writing to every residents association, you could simply log in to Profile and ask for information on residents associations which had been covered in the UK national press. You would then be told within about 15 seconds how much coverage there had been. You could then sort this coverage into date order and get the database to send you all the relevant text. For half a dozen different articles this would take about 10 minutes and would cost you £25 plus the cost of your local telephone call.

For information about contacting Profile call:

British Telecom
Network House
Brindley Way
Hemel Hempstead
Herts HP3 9RR
Tel: 01442 237237

Compuserve
Compuserve is an American database, though it does have an
important European centre of information. This database has all
sorts of information including up to the minute weather satellite
data, US stock price information and travel booking facilities. The
cost of Compuserve varies according to the option you choose.

To contact Compuserve you can call: 0800 289558.

The Internet
This is a worldwide collection of databases and information
systems all connected together. No-one owns the Internet and you
can join in the system from literally hundreds of connection
services. The best way is to get one of the many Internet magazines
and check out your local Internet connection.

How do I access the databases?
To access these databases you will also need a modem, which is a
device that allows your computer to be connected to the telephone
system. These vary in price from £100 to £1,000: the higher the
price the more features you get and the faster the work is processed.
If you get a slow modem you will only have higher telephone bills!
So, choose a modem which is fast and be prepared to spend around
£300 for a good, reliable model.

To work out the costs of using databases you will need to make
some estimates. You first need to estimate how much of your
publication's information will depend on database sourcing. Then
you will need to estimate how many minutes you will need to use
the database to extract the information. This is a bit awkward until
you know exactly how these databases work and how much
information you extract. However, if you estimate that to get the
information for half a page of an A4 newsletter will take 15 minutes
on-line you will not be too far out when it comes to working out
your likely costs.

Fill in the following table to estimate your on-line database costs.

Table 6

Database	Registration fee	Connection hours	Connection fee

Television

Television is a wonderful source of ideas and information. If you produce a newsletter you will often be sitting at home in front of the box when you realise that the programme you are watching has included something of interest to your readers. But television is now a 24-hour operation: if programmes containing information of interest to your readers are on during the day, how will you get that information? You may need a TV in your office or a video recorder to catch those interesting snippets. A good idea is to buy a combination TV and video which will cost around £450. These items will cost money. You will also need a television licence for the office as the one you have at home will not cover your business TV.

Table 7

Cost of equipment needed	£
TV licence fee	£
Total	£

Radio

Like TV, radio programmes can also be a useful source of information for your newsletter. You may need a radio in your office and a cassette recorder to record the material you are interested in. Fortunately you do not need a licence to listen to the radio, so at least one expense is saved. Nevertheless, you can't watch TV, listen to the radio, edit your newsletter and do the rest of your work all at the same time. You may need to consider paying someone to monitor broadcasts for you. If you really want this job done to the utmost degree you can get specialist services of broadcast monitors who check programmes to see if anything of interest to your requirements was broadcast. They then send you a written transcript. The service is available from companies like The Broadcast Monitoring Company on 0171-833 1055.

Fill in the following table to calculate your radio costs.

Table 8

Cost of radio/cassette recorder	£
Estimated monitoring fees per year	£
Total	£

Interviews

Many newsletters contain profiles of people or interviews with leading experts seeking their views on some important topic. Getting such interviews will cost money. You should use the same calculation as for press conferences to work out how much these items will cost. Again expect to use one main interview per issue. If you haven't bought a tape recorder for radio programmes you will certainly need one for interviews, so this could be another cost. Some interviewees also like to be paid for their views. This is not accepted practice and is generally frowned upon by most writers; after all, the interview is essentially providing free publicity. However, some film and television stars demand fees for interviews (or at least their agents do) and many politicians get paid TV appearance fees, so they could well ask for a fee for their time. Mostly you will not be asked, but it may be worthwhile budgeting a small amount for the eventuality, say up to £300 for one in twenty interviews.

The following table should allow you to work out your interview costs.

Table 9

Costs of attending interviews per year	£
Price of tape recorder	£
Likely interview fees	£
Total costs of interviews	£

Anonymous tip-offs

These are the sort of information sources you see in films about the media. Some hack is sitting puffing away at a cigarette, with a bottle of whisky beside the typewriter when the phone rings. A gruff voice announces something vital and then . . . the dialling tone. The journalist doesn't know who called, but sure knows the information is important.

Sometimes newsletter editors do get anonymous tip-offs, but usually they do not. Indeed, few journalists receive them. Far too many people ring up newspapers in the mistaken belief they will get paid for their, usually ill-informed, material. There are some anonymous tip-offs, though, but they do cost money. For a start you need a telephone line to get the information, and you need to publicise the number. However, the costs of tip-offs can thankfully be borne by your promotion costs (see page 62).

Table 10

Annual cost of publications	£
Annual cost of personal contacts	£
Annual cost of using PR agencies	£
Annual cost of press releases	£
Annual cost of press conferences	£
Annual cost of computer databases	£
Annual cost of television	£
Annual cost of radio	£
Annual cost of interviews	£
Total information gathering costs	£

Total costs of information gathering

Now you can work out exactly how much it will cost you each year to gather information for your newsletter. All you need to do is enter the totals from Tables 1 to 9 in Table 10 on page 51.

WRITING COSTS

Writing is big business. There are thousands of people across the country whose only source of income is writing. They can earn potentially huge sums and some well-known authors can get seven figure sums for the sales of their books. If you want someone like that to write the words for your newsletter you are going to have to pay handsomely for them.

Who should do the writing?

Who actually writes the words for your newsletter will be down to a combination of factors, but don't forget to take into account the needs and expectations of your audience. If the look and feel of the publication is just right, you will simply alienate your readers if the writing is rotten. In spite of what you may think, writing is not a gift. It is not some talent from on high bestowed on just a few selected mortals; anyone can learn to write. There are some simple techniques in Chapter 5, and you can learn more from *How to Write for Publication*, by Chriss McCallum, in this series. Another important book to look for is *How to Write and Speak Better* by the Readers Digest. There are plenty of books which advise you on how to write good copy. But don't forget to include the costs in your budget if you need to buy these books.

What's the cost?

If you think you can write the material for your newsletter your only cost will be your time. However, if you need expert assistance or specialist support you will need to employ the services of freelance writers. How to locate good contributors is covered in Chapter 4. Here we need to work out how much they will cost you.

Most freelance writers will work out their charges according to the number of words they provide. Generally, freelance fees are quoted 'per thousand words'. Some of the more business-like freelance writers charge by the hour, rather like a solicitor does, and will tell you how many hours a particular task will take so you know how much an article will cost.

The charges per thousand words vary enormously. Some writers are happy to accept £50 for 1,000 words, that's about four to five sides of A4 paper typed in double spacing. Other writers will not work for less than £600 per 1,000 words. In general, you will find it hard to employ good writers for anything less than £150 per 1,000 words. For most newsletters this means you would be paying around £100 per published A4 page.

For writers who charge by the hour the rates vary from £10 to £75 per hour. Some of the top professionals charge even more and quote a figure of around £1,000 per day. Generally an average of £30 per hour appears to be the current norm for good writers at present. In most instances this means you will again need to budget around £100 per printed page as a writer would average 750 words in three to four hours, including basic research and telephone calls.

So to work out your writing costs you need to do the following calculation:

No of printed pages x 100 x No of issues/year

You will also need to provide the writers with copies of your newsletter and the information you want them to convert to prose, so there will be some costs involved in doing this. A rough estimate will be £10 per issue per writer.

To work out the total costs of your writing complete the following table.

Table 11

Cost of written material per year	£
Costs of informing writers per year	£
Total costs of writing	£

EDITING COSTS

As already explained, editing involves a great deal more than making everything fit. Editing is a skilled job and unless you have experience or are willing to learn you could easily find that your publication loses appeal because you are not continuing to match readers' expectations.

Who should edit it?

You can learn to edit. Every editor in the land had to learn. It is not that you can't edit, you just haven't learned yet. Naturally, this book will help you edit, but if you really want to learn you should go on a training course. Some of the best courses to suit newsletter editors are run by The British Association of Communicators in Business. This is an organisation representing all of the people who produce newsletters, magazines, etc. for British based industry and commerce. If you intend producing a company newsletter or staff magazine you should join. The Association is also one of the UK's premier training organisations for people producing newsletters and the like. For more information on the courses and the Association contact:

3 Locks Yard
High Street
Sevenoaks
Kent TN13 1LT
Tel: 01732 459331

The Association is also a useful source of freelance editors. There are also plenty of firms, like the one I run, ASPECT, which specialise in editing newsletters for clients. If you decide that you do not wish to edit your own newsletter just yet, you can enlist the services of a freelance editor to do the work for you to your strict brief. The charges will vary, but expect to pay around £30 per hour. You will need to discuss how many hours the job is likely to take, but for an 8-page newsletter you could expect a professional editor to do the work required in around 16 hours. Allow two hours per page and you should be in the right region. These charges do not take into account design and production costs which are dealt with later in this chapter.

If you really feel you cannot afford freelance editors then do not despair at these prices. You might be putting together a local newsletter for your drama society and the help of a freelance editor could be beyond your budgets at this stage, but there are always other people willing to help on a voluntary basis or for a smaller fee. Whatever you do, though, do not ask the local English teacher. Many local newsletters think that someone who understands the English language is the best kind of editor. They are usually the worst! They are far too interested in the structure of the language, the beauty of the discourse or the wonderment of the similes. They all too easily forget things like deadlines, making the articles fit, and making them readable to everyone, whether or not they have a degree in English Literature! I know this is a generalisation, but be warned. People who understand literature are not always the best individuals to help you with your editing.

Why not try using a reporter or sub-editor from the local paper? These journalists are often willing to help give advice and encouragement. They could assist in your editing and will be useful in getting publicity about your organisation as well. These people will be glad of the experience and will not be likely to charge you the £30 per hour of full-time freelance editors.

To work out the cost of editing complete the following table.

Table 12

Cost of training courses	£
Cost of freelance editing for year	£
Entertainment expenses for freelance editor	£
Total costs of editing	£

DESIGN COSTS

The cost of design can be as high as you want. You can get designers who charge phenomenal amounts of money, several thousands of pounds per day. You can also get designers who will do the work for a few pints down the local. The choice is yours. For historical reasons, mainly, design tends to be more expensive than either editing or writing. Another reason is that the design of each issue is the single most striking aspect of your newsletter. If the design is poor the reaction from readers will be negative, no matter how good the words or how brilliantly edited the whole publication.

How can I find out more?

Design is a complex subject. If you want to know more than I cover in this book, you should read *Publication Design* by Roy Paul Newson (see Further Information p. 169). Large bookshops such as Dillons in London import these sort of books. You could also try the following company:

Graphics Books International
PO Box 349
Lowlands
Vale
Guernsey
Channel Islands
Tel: 01481 48181

This is a mail order supplier of graphics, design and publishing books and provides a free book-like catalogue.

Also, if you want to learn newsletter design with individual tuition, contact:

The Newsletter School
ASPECT
PO Box 43
Thatcham
Berkshire RG19 4WH

You can also learn design skills with the British Association of Communicators in Business and if you use electronic methods of publishing you can get design courses from:

PPA
Silwood Park
Ascot
Berkshire SL5 4PW
Tel: 01344 25543

To work out your design costs complete the following table:

Table 13

Cost of design training courses	£
Cost of design books	£
Cost of freelance design for year	£
Cost of entertaining freelance designer	£
Total costs of design	£

TYPESETTING COSTS

What is it and what will I need?

By typesetting I mean anything from basic typewriting to full commercial typesetting. It is unlikely that any newsletter producer is going to buy their own typesetting equipment. My organisation produces dozens of newsletters and it is still cheaper for me to hire typesetting, rather than buy my own equipment. Only for very large corporations where the cost of purchasing the equipment could be spread across a variety of projects would it be worth considering.

The equipment you are likely to buy, though, is either some kind of typewriter, or a computer capable of 'desktop publishing'. The equipment you need will be determined by the psychological profiling you did earlier on. In the past, many newsletters were produced using typewriters. Nowadays, they are the minority and most newsletters use desktop publishing equipment.

Once you have bought your computer you will need to budget for training courses. PPA, mentioned earlier, trains people to use DTP equipment of all kinds as do other training organisations. Most of the companies offering training advertise in computer magazines like *MacUser, PC User* and *Personal Computer World*. All of these are available at newsagents. In general you will need around two to three days of training to 'get going', followed up by a couple of days more in-depth training at a later date. Each day of training will cost you around £200.

What will it cost?

The material you produce from your desktop publishing equipment can either be laser printed or a disk can be sent to a typesetting bureau who can produce the high quality originals required for offset litho printing. If you intend producing more than a couple of hundred copies or more than a two-page newsletter, using a bureau and a commercial printer will be cheaper than a laser printer. However, for small newsletter projects you can run off the copies direct on the laser printer of your desktop publishing system. Naturally, each copy will cost something to print, and taking into account the amount of electricity used, the toner ink used, the cost of each sheet of 100gsm paper and the time your laser printer is employed doing the work you should allow 0.75p per copy as your actual costs. (Note that if you do not have a laser printer and go to a company which does have one you will be charged between 75p and £2 for a page.)

If you want typeset output from your disks you will be charged between £1 and £10 per page depending on the size of the page and the quality of the output you require.

So to work out your costs of typesetting you need to do the following calculation:

Price per page x No of pages/issue x No of issues/year

If you only want to use a typewriter you will need to calculate the cost of ribbons, paper and any special typeface disks or golfballs that you buy.

To calculate your total typesetting costs complete the table on page 59.

PRINTING COSTS

You cannot avoid printing costs. Even if you are producing a small newsletter for a few friends you will need to pay for the photo-copying. If you are producing a glossy colour newsletter for your staff, you certainly will need to pay for printing.

How much should I pay?

There is no easy way to calculate your printing price. You should

Table 14

Cost of typewriter	£
Cost of computer and laser printer	£
Cost of desktop publishing programs	£
Cost of training courses	£
Cost of laser printing/year	£
Cost of bereau service/year	£
Total costs of typesetting	£

get at least three quotations from local printers; you will find quite a wide variation. The most expensive price will be from a company that does not want the work! The least costly will often be from companies which really need the job. Going for a mid-range price is usually the safest. But you will need to consider how far away the printer is from you and how much it will cost to get your typesetting to the printing company.

To get the best price give your printer as much information as possible. Fortunately, you will have compiled most of the information your printer requires in Chapter 2. The Look and Feel Plan is just what your printer will need to help estimate the price. In addition the printer will need to know how many copies you want printed. You should also let your printer know that you intend to supply 'CRC', which means **camera ready copy**. One other thing is that you will need to say roughly how many photos will be included and whether they will be in colour or black and white. Use the form in Figure 1 for asking for quotations from printers. Then multiply the printing price you select by the number of issues per year to get your annual print price.

Please provide a written estimate for printing the following:	
Title	
Material to be supplied	
Trimmed page size	
Number of pages	
Type of paper	
Number of colours	
Print run	
Run-on	
Binding	
Finishing	
Delivery date	
Special requests	

Fig. 1.   Form to request printer's quote.

Now complete the table below to calculate your annual costs of printing:

Table 15

Annual cost of printing/photocopying	£
Transport/courier costs for delivery of artwork to printer	£
Total printing cost	£

DISTRIBUTION COSTS

Distribution is a key element of the success of your newsletter. If you can't get copies to your audience, they can't read it. Issue two would never be produced!

There are various forms of distribution. The main ones for newsletters are:

- hand delivery
- mailing
- bulk dropping.

Delivered newsletters are either handed out at meetings or popped through the reader's letterbox. Mailed newsletters are sent direct to the readers via the postal system. Bulk drops are often used by staff newsletters; piles of copies are placed in strategic places, like canteens and staff rooms, for readers to pick up. The type of distribution you use will depend upon the expectations of your readers and how important the information is. For instance, some newsletters in the City are distributed daily by fax.

What costs are involved?

If you distribute by mail you will need to calculate the cost of each envelope, each stamp, each label and the 'stuffing' of the envelopes (placing the newsletter inside the envelope). A mailing company would charge around 45p for each envelope to do all this work.

You then need to do the following calculation for a mailed newsletter:

Cost per cenvelope x No of copies to be mailed x No of issues per year

If you intend bulk dropping to a number of sites you will need to provide for any transport costs and the payment of any staff to do the deliveries.

If you distribute by hand you may well need to pay a small fee to the people who drop the newsletters through letterboxes. Local freesheet newspapers pay in the region of £2.50 per 100 delivered.

To calculate the annual cost of distributing your newsletter complete the following table:

Table 16

Cost of annual mailing	£
Cost of transport for bulk mailings	£
Fees due to hand delivery agents	£
Total cost of distribution	£

PROMOTIONAL COSTS

No matter how good your newsletter, how closely it matches your psychological profiles and how much value for money you provide, people will not read your newsletter if they don't know about it. You need to promote your newsletter to attract new readers and to maintain the loyalty of existing readers.

How do I do it?

There is not enough space in this book to go into details about promoting your newsletter, but you will need to consider the following types of promotion:

● advertising

- direct mail
- public relations
- sales promotion efforts
- exhibitions
- promotional talks.

More details on many of these items can be found in other *How To* books including *How to Start a Business from Home, How to Do Your Own Advertising* and *How to Do Your Own PR*. You will also find *Business to Business Marketing* by Martyn P Davis, published by Business Books Ltd, a useful guide.

Carefully cost the amount you will need to spend on promoting your newsletter and enter the figures in the table below.

Table 17

Cost of advertising	£
Cost of direct mail	£
Cost of public relations	£
Cost of sales promotions	£
Cost of exhibitions	£
Cost of talks	£
Total annual cost of promotion	£

TOTAL ANNUAL COSTS

The moment of truth

Now that you have completed all your calculations you can work out exactly how much money you need to finance your newsletter for its first year. Simply enter the totals from Table 10 to Table 17 in Table 18 on the next page.

Table 18

Annual cost of information gathering	£
Annual cost of writing	£
Annual cost of editing	£
Annual cost of design	£
Annual cost of typesetting	£
Annual cost of printing	£
Annual cost of distribution	£
Annual cost of promotion	£
Total annual cost of producing newsletter	£
Now add 10% just to be sure!	£

INCOME

The total annual cost of your newsletter can be anything from as little as £10 to as much as £1m depending on who you are and the type of newsletter you want to produce. In either case you will want to be able to generate some income for your newsletter.

Types of income
You can get income from a variety of sources. These are:

- subscriptions
- advertising
- reader services
- grants
- donations.

Subscriptions

If you are to offer high value news which cannot be obtained quickly elsewhere and is of interest to businesses, you can charge a premium price. *Scrip*, for example, is a newsletter for the pharmaceutical industry published by PJB Publications of Richmond, Surrey. The newsletter comes out 100 times a year and costs £275 per annum. The monthly newsletter on desktop publishing from Seybold publications in America costs $210 per year for just 12 issues.

If you wish to charge a subscription make sure it is the right market price. Check the prices of other publications to see that you are in the right area. Do not simply divide your annual costs by the number of issues you have a year to come out with your cover price. You could be too cheap!

Don't forget that many newsletters are free. Your colleagues in the bowls club will not be too happy if you present them with a bill for £150 a year for their club newsletter!

Advertising

Virtually every newsletter can benefit from advertising. Whether you produce a newsletter for your customers or a big colour newsletter for your staff you can accept adverts. The price you charge for adverts will depend on:

- your circulation
- the style of your newsletter
- the number of issues per year
- whether you use colour.

To work out the potential income from your adverts get the 'rate cards' of similar publications. These are available from the advertising departments and you can get their telephone numbers from:

The Advertisers Annual
Windsor Court
East Grinstead House
East Grinstead
West Sussex RH19 1XA
Tel: 01342 326972

Willings Press Guide
Reed Information Services
Windsor Court
East Grinstead House
East Grinstead
West Sussex Rh19 1XA
Tel: 01342 326972

Benns Media Directory
PO Box 20
Sovereign Way
Tonbridge
Kent TN9 1RQ
Tel: 01732 362666

By looking at the rate cards you will be able to see the sort of prices you can charge. However, do not think that advertising will flood in. You will need to spend a great deal of effort in trying to attract advertisers, and of all the potential advertisers you should expect to only get one in every 100 actually buying space in your newsletter.

Reader services
You can always get some money from providing services to your readers. Say you produce a newsletter for your local tennis club; you can earn some money by providing tennis balls and clothing at discount prices. You can get the things to sell from a local wholesaler who will knock down the costs a bit because of the amount you sell and the direct line you have to an eager audience. You can mark up the prices by less than a normal retailer, so providing the service of a discount to your readers while still making some profit.

Other services you can consider are advice and consultancy, or holidays, trips and outings. The services you provide will depend on the type of newsletter you produce and the expectations of your audience. But don't neglect services, they are a very useful way of earning some income.

Grants
If you produce a newsletter of particular special interest you may

be eligible for a grant. They are available from local authorities and the EU. You can get further details from:

The European Investment Bank
68 Pall Mall
London SW1Y 5ES
Tel: 0171-839 3351

Donations
You may find a benefactor for your newsletter. Sponsorship of newsletters is widespread, but be wary. Sponsors may often want some degree of editorial control, so if you don't want this be careful of who you ask for donations. People willing to donate to newsletters include businesses, local dignitaries, etc.

Table 19

Annual income from subscriptions	£
Annual income from advertising	£
Annual income from reader services	£
Annual income from grants	£
Annual income from donors/sponsors	£
Subtotal A	£
Annual cost of selling advertising	£
Cost of reference books for advertising	£
Cost of entertaining sponsors	£
Subtotal B	£
Total annual income (A—B)	

Total income

To calculate your total likely income for your newsletter complete Table 19 on page 67.

Now that you know how much income you can get from your newsletter, and how much it will cost, you will be able to see if the project will make a profit or a loss. If it is profitable, all well and good. If the newsletter will make a loss this may not be a bad thing. If it is for a group or association, the funds of the organisation may make up the difference. If the newsletter is a business one for customers or staff, you can get the difference made up by money from the publicity budget. If, however, your newsletter is to be a commercial venture, do not start it if it is likely to make a loss. Even if things improve in later years, the lack of income in the first year will be difficult to make up.

If a loss is shown in your budgeting then look again at your plans. See if your reader expectations can be met by another format, or with fewer editions per year. Don't compromise on quality, but look at ways you can alter your plans to reduce your costs or increase your income. Things you might consider are:

- reducing the number of issues
- reducing the number of pages
- reducing the number of colours
- increasing the price of subscriptions
- increasing the price of adverts
- increasing the range of reader services.

A SAMPLE BUDGET: THE STUDENT UNION

The Millchester Student Union has done its planning well and produced the following financial statement for its proposed fortnightly newsletter:

Costs

Cost of information gathering

Publications	£117
Personal contacts	£150
PR agencies	£50

Press releases	—
Press conferences	—
Computer databases	£120
Television	—
Radio	£25
Interviews	—
TOTAL	£462

Cost of writing and editing

Training	£250
Freelance help, local reporter	£300
TOTAL	£550

Cost of design

Training	£400
Books	£75
TOTAL	£475

Cost of typesetting

Laser printed originals	£2
TOTAL	£2

Cost of printing

Litho printing	£4,500
TOTAL	£4,500

Cost of distribution

Bulk dropping	—

Cost of promotion

Posters on campus	£150

TOTAL ANNUAL COST	£6,139

Income

Subscriptions to former students	£500
Advertising	£4,125
Reader services (T-shirts, records)	£1,200

TOTAL ANNUAL INCOME	£5,825

There is a shortfall of £314 which the Union President has agreed to provide from Student Union funds. This is equivalent to a funding of less than 1/100th of a pence per copy printed since we will print 45,000 copies over the coming year (3,000 issued on 15 occasions).

The lessons learned
This detailed budgetary plan which does not show the workings-out, is just the sort of thing you need to prepare. No matter what type of newsletter you need to produce, its continued success depends upon sound financial planning at the outset. To help you complete your financial plan use the form in Figure 2 to enter your own figures.

ANNUAL BUDGETING

Although this chapter has worked through the steps necessary for you to ensure that your newsletter can get off the ground in the first instance, do not neglect annual budgeting. Print prices will change each year, as will distribution costs, so be sure to revise your budgets every year to make sure that your newsletter is still viable.

EXPENDITURE	£	INCOME	£
INFORMATION		SUBSCRIPTIONS	
Publications		ADVERTISEMENTS	
Contacts		Classifieds	
PR		Display	
Press releases		READER SERVICES	
Press conferences		GRANTS	
Databases		DONATIONS	
TV		TOTAL INCOME	£
Radio			
Interviews			
WRITING			
Commissioning fees			
Informing writers			
EDITING			
Training			
Freelancers			
Books			
Entertainment			
TYPESETTING			
Equipment			
Bureau services			
PRINTING			
Photocopying			
Commercial printing			
Couriers			
DISTRIBUTION			
Envelopes			
Postage			
Transport			
Agents' fees			
PROMOTION			
Advertising			
Direct mail			
PR			
Sales promotion			
Exhibitions			
Talks		INCOME MINUS	
TOTAL EXPENDITURE	£	EXPENDITURE	£

Fig. 2. Financial plan for a newsletter.

4
Editing Your Newsletter

In the last chapter you saw how much the various information sources available to you would cost. You also gained some insight as to which ones are most likely to be useful to you. This chapter explains how to select good contributors for your newsletter. In addition you will learn how to **edit** your newsletter.

THE EDITING PROCESS

Editing, as already explained, is more than just gathering material and fitting it onto the available pages. It consists of a whole host of tasks which allow your newsletter to match the expectations of your target audience, thus ensuring high levels of readership. Editing is also about establishing a relationship with readers so that you can get constant feedback on your newsletter and therefore mould it to the growing needs of your audience. If the newsletter does not adapt itself over time you will not be keeping up with the changing psychological profile of your readers. As a result you will lose readership and your newsletter will die a slow, painful death.

To ensure that your newsletter is successful you need to do the tasks listed below in your editing work. These tasks have become known as '**the editing process**' and take place on every newspaper and magazine in the land.

Editing tasks

- establish reader profile
- structure the newsletter
- construct copy flow plan
- commission written contributions
- commission illustrations
- read contributions

- select illustrations
- copy edit contributions
- fit copy
- lay out page
- subedit
- write headlines
- proof read
- stone subbing
- gather feedback
- establish reader profile.

As you can see, the editing process starts and finishes with the same task, establishing your reader profile. If you have worked through the steps in this book so far, you will have already produced a fairly detailed psychological profile of your likely readers. If you have not done this, do it now. You will not be able to perform the other editing tasks successfully without that written profile in your hands. Notice that when you have finished editing your first issue, your next editing task is to re-assess that readership profile so that you can ensure your second issue will also be a success.

STRUCTURING THE NEWSLETTER

Your newsletter is bound to fail if it does not have a structure. Many people who put newsletters together simply place the material on the pages without giving any thought to where items should go, their relative importance and so on. Readers require a 'route map' to enable them to see their way clearly through your newsletter. Without a coherent and consistent structure, your newsletters will be like trying to wade your way through an overgrown wood in the middle of the night.

Take a look at your favourite daily newspaper. The main news items are always on the first few pages; then there may be a couple of pages of foreign news, next the paper's editorial column, then perhaps the TV page and the theatre reviews, before the stars and the cartoons come. Each issue is structured identically. Everyone who reads the *Daily Mail* knows the TV programmes are always after the centre pages; for readers of the *Guardian* the 'comment' section is always inside the back cover. This regularity breeds familiarity; readers feel comfortable and they do not have to search for items in which they are interested.

A regular and consistent structure to your newsletter is vital. Your readers will be able to find their way around much more easily if they know where items will be.

Case study: The estate agent

Tony Smythe has reconsidered his newsletter and has realised that he was forced to scrap the idea because of his poor preparation and lack of financial planning. He has now decided to start the newsletter again, this time with a proper plan and budget. He has also called in the help of his friend, Michael Arlington, the Property Editor of the local newspaper in nearby Goldmead.

Michael has told Tony that his newsletter needs a clear structure. The two of them have worked out the following basic structure into which the editorial matter they wish to publish will always fit:

Page 1	Village news
Page 2	Property news
Page 3	Planning news
Page 4	Parish council column
Page 5	Village personality profile
Page 6	Goldmead Focus
Page 7	Political columns
Page 8	Village sports news

Tony now knows what he has to include and therefore knows how much material he wants on what topics for each issue. His readers are also satisfied because they always know, for instance, that if they want to read what their local councillors are up to they will find the information on page 7.

Case study: The student union

The student union at Millchester has been following the path to success for its newsletter, so it comes as no surprise that Steve Wilson, who is putting together the publication, has produced the following plan:

Page 1	Union news
Page 2	University news
Page 3	Sports news
Page 4	What's on column

You will notice that both structures have the most important category at the front, with a similarly important category on the back. In an eight-page newsletter there is also a fairly important category in the centre. Reading surveys have shown that if you want to convey important information, put it on the front, back or centre of your publication. If these areas are already taken up then put the important material in the first few pages of the newsletter. The last half of your newsletter will always attract fewer readers, so do not put vitally important material in this section. Include material here which may be of interest to just some people in your reader profile.

CONSTRUCTING A COPY FLOW PLAN

So now you know what categories of information you are going to include in your newsletter and where those items will appear. You cannot just sit back, though, and hope that enough items come in to fill the relevant pages; you would wait forever. Editors have to manage the flow of information into their publication, otherwise it would not be produced on time. As already mentioned in Chapter 2, your newsletter must come out regularly to ensure continued readership. If your newsletter is produced on an ad-hoc basis you will certainly lose readers.

If you want your newsletter to be published on regular dates you need to ensure that you get your written contributions by specific dates. To work out this date you need to know how long the editing and printing will take. So to work out your copy flow plan, first you need a 'schedule'.

Schedule

Your schedule must always begin with the date you want copies in the hands of your readers and work backwards from that point. The following case history shows how this works.

Case history: The estate agent

Tony Smythe has decided to publish six of his newsletters a year. He wants his readers to receive issues on the first day of February, April, June, August, October, and December. This means he needs to hand over the copies to his delivery agents (his office assistants) on the 28th of the previous months so that there is time for these people to get round all the houses. To do that, the printer would need to deliver the items on the 27th, which means they would need the artwork by the 20th of that month to give them time to do the printing. Tony realises that the artwork would take two days to produce, which means the typesetting bureau must have his disk on the 17th of the month preceding 'publication'. Tony knows it will take two days to do the proof reading and the corrections, so the final version needs to be ready by the 15th. The page layout will take Michael from Goldmead some three days, so all of the edited material and pictures need to be available by the 12th. Tony reckons it will take him four evenings to go through the contributions and choose the pictures, so he needs to start work on this by the 8th of each month, which means he needs all of the articles from his contributors by the 6th, to be safe. Considering it is likely to take a couple of weeks for his contributors to find material for their articles, he needs to commission them on the 24th of the previous month.

For the April issue his schedule was:

- Commission writers   24th February

- Contributions to Tony Smythe   6th March

- Edited contributions/illustrations
  to Michael Arlington   12th March

- Page layouts to Tony Smythe   15th March

- Proofreading and corrections by   17th March

- Disk to typesetter   18th March

- Artwork to printer by   20th March

- Delivery from printers to Tony Smythe 27th March

- Hand over to distribution agents   28th March

- Delivery to readers   29th-31st March

Your schedule

To develop your schedule, work out how long each of the tasks will take to perform. Then start at the bottom of the schedule with the delivery date to your readers and work upwards from that point. You will then know when you must start doing the commissioning.

COMMISSIONING WRITTEN CONTRIBUTIONS

Many newsletter editors simply say to potential contributors that if they have anything of interest, send it in when they get a chance. Invariably, no one sends a word, the editor complains that it is impossible to produce the newsletter without any articles and gives up. Usually, the editor will make a few valiant attempts and write the entire publication from cover to cover, but this begins to wear after a while and the job appears to be more than it's worth. This is typical of many newsletters, even 'professional' newsletters produced in-house for staff or customers.

The very real fact of life is that nobody will write anything for your newsletter unless you make them! Unless they are journalists employed by your company to prepare text for the in-house newsletter, you will not get more than a couple of hand scrawled titbits.

How do you go about commissioning?

The first step is to look back at your structure plan for the newsletter. You can see at an instant what topics you want covered. The next stage is to select individuals who can produce articles for the categories of your structure. Who writes the material depends on your budgets and your individual circumstances. If yours is a small newsletter for a club or association you will need to identify members who have particular knowledge of the topics you want covered. If yours is a large, colour newsletter, you may be able to afford professional freelance writers. (See Chapter 3 for the costs.)

Using freelance writers
Finding the right colleague or friend to do the writing is relatively easy. Finding a freelance is not so easy. The National Union of Journalists publishes a director of freelances and there is also *The Publishers Directory* which lists freelance writers and their specialist areas. In addition there are a number of specialist writers associations, like the British Guild of Travel Writers or the Medical Journalists Association, which can provide lists of freelance contributors. You can get the details of such associations from the *Writers' and Artists' Yearbook*. You can also get freelance writers from the British Association of Communicators in Business.

To select the best contributor for your newsletter ask to see cuttings of work the writer has done before. If they are professional you will get an assortment of clippings so that you can see the topics the journalist has covered and the style of their writing. Ask the freelance if they have done the kind of work you want before, and if so get any details. Also ask them to send their CV so you can see who they've written for and for how long. All of this information will help you select the right freelance contributor.

Once you have selected your contributors you can now ask them to do the work you request. If you are using freelancers this is easy. You simply call them, tell them exactly what it is you want written, how many words you want (see Copy Fitting in this chapter) and the date you want the material (the deadline). You then negotiate the fee and off they go. You should be clear about **copyright** and **contracts**, though. Details of these are found in Chapter 9, but at this stage you should realise that for the rates discussed in Chapter 3 you will not be buying all the rights in the articles you commission. Much higher fees are charged for that and there has to be a written contract explaining such. What you buy from most freelance writers is the right to use the words they write once and once only in a single edition of one publication. That is not the problem that at first sight it seems; a fuller discussion is in Chapter 9. At the time of commissioning, though, it is important to discuss the copyright you expect, as this will have cost implications.

Using non-professional writers
If you are commissioning material from fellow club members or employees of your company, the procedure is much the same. You tell them what you want, the number of words you need and the deadline. In most instances you will not be paying these contributors. However, if you give them fancy titles, like 'Sports Correspondent', or whatever, these people feel part of your team, they know their name will be printed and they get a boost to their ego. By appointing your colleagues and co-members as 'specialist correspondents' they will be far more likely to meet their deadlines and produce your contributions. However, if you can afford it, payment will certainly elicit the copy faster!

COMMISSIONING ILLUSTRATIONS

Essentially, commissioning illustrations is much the same as for written contributions. You need to select the illustrator with care, tell them exactly what you want, and when you need it. You may also need to talk about payments and copyright. Like writers, photographers retain the copyright in all the pictures they take, unless an alternative written agreement is signed. (See Chapter 9 for more details.)

Say what you want
The one thing that is different about commissioning illustrations is the degree of specificity you need to give. You have to say exactly what you want. If you want a picture of the local church, don't just ask a friend to take one. Say that you want a picture of the church, showing the golden angel on the clock tower, taken at dusk so the sun is behind the tower, in colour, on 35mm slide film. Good professional photographers will ask you plenty of questions, but if you need to use keen amateurs do say exactly what you want. If you do not know what you want, explain to the photographer or artist what you are illustrating and be happy to show them the article, if you have it. This will help the illustrator work out what you need.

To find photographers, look in the *NUJ Freelance Directory*, the *Publishers' Handbook* and in the *Hollis Directory*. You will also see photographers listed in *Yellow Pages*, but be sure to check their credentials. Many are wedding photographers, and taking pictures of a family group is entirely different to getting shots of your football team in action. If in any doubt about photographers, speak to the photography department of your local newspaper.

READING CONTRIBUTIONS

This is vital and judging by many newsletters I have seen is one the most forgotten stages of the editing process. Getting the right contributor and ensuring they get the material to you on time is all very well, but simply including every word they have written without passing judgement is not on. You are the only person who knows your reader profile inside out. You must check every contribution to ensure that it will have instant appeal to your readers. You must also make sure that your contributions tickle the main emotions you are targeting. If the material that has been contributed does not provide what you wanted, get the writer to do the work again, or re-write what has been submitted.

Is it all right to make changes?

If, however, the article is basically acceptable but needs some minor alterations, change the words yourself. Do not think that writers, particularly full time professionals, are upset by your changes. They expect them. No matter how much care a writer has taken there are bound to be flaws. Proper editing improves a writer's words, so full time professionals are pleased to accept changes. It is the amateurs you have to watch! If you enlist colleagues or fellow club members to write articles for you, they are likely to take some offence if you change what they have written. The way around this is to explain at the outset that you have final say over what goes in your newsletter and that whilst you are very grateful for their contributions there may be occasions when you need to alter things a bit to allow enough space for other articles, or to adjust things for balance depending upon what else is included. Most amateur contributors will accept this kind of tactful approach and will privately, at least, be grateful you changed their rubbish to something much more polished and still put their name at the top!

SELECTING ILLUSTRATIONS

In the same way that you must go through the articles carefully, you must also take your time over pictures. It is no good simply accepting the first picture someone sends to you for your newsletter. Indeed, professionals will send you a selection, so if you are

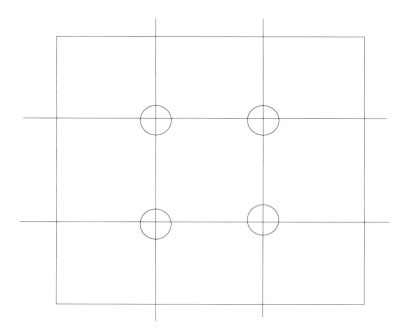

Fig. 3. The main point of interest in an illustration should be within one of the circled areas.

using keen amateurs be sure to ask them to take at least half a dozen different shots to give you something to choose from.

Selecting an illustration will depend on a variety of factors, including your own subjective impression. However, the most important factor to think about is the rule of thirds. Psychological research has shown that our interest in a picture is much higher if the main feature is in one of four positions, as shown in Figure 3.

COPY EDITING CONTRIBUTIONS

This is a vital part of the editing process. You will have read the articles once and made any major changes necessary. Now you must go through the articles with a fine tooth comb. You need to check for the following features:

- profile
- logic
- accuracy

- consistency

- house style

- balance

- legality.

Profile

Go through the copy and check that the article fits the psychological profile of your newsletter readers. If not, make changes.

Logic

You should go through each article and see if it makes sense. Does what the writer has written convey a meaningful message? Or doesn't it make sense? If the article is in any way confusing, change it.

Accuracy

Check the facts. If the article mentions some factual point, check it. If, for instance, the writer has said there have been 200 road accidents in the county this year, is that right? Should it have been 2,000 or 20? Could a typing error have occurred? Check material facts and ensure they are right.

Consistency

Has the author been consistent? If the writer has called someone Mr Jenkinson throughout the article, why change it to John, in the last paragraph? If the amounts of cows milk drunk a year are quoted in litres, why is petrol used given in gallons? Check that figures, names and other details are used consistently. If they are not, you will confuse the readers and slowly lose their loyalty.

House style

Every newsletter should have its own **house style**. This is discussed in more detail in the next chapter, but for the moment you need to be sure that the articles you edit follow your house style rules. If, for instance, you always use USA, you cannot accept United States. If you always call the chief executive by his full name and title, don't accept a contribution where he is referred to by his first name. Your newsletter should have rules about many items and in copy editing you need to check that the rules have been obeyed.

Balance
Is the article balanced? If it presents two sides of an argument, have both sides been given fair treatment? If the article is one-sided, is that acceptable or do you need another article to redress the balance? Your readers will expect your publication to be provocative and thought provoking, but they will not like it if it is unfair. You must be seen to be fair, so you must check every item of copy for balance.

Legality
Check each contribution with care to see if it breaks any laws. Is the text potentially libellous? Or has the author infringed copyright by quoting people or other material? **Libel** and **copyright** are explained in more detail in Chapter 9. The point to remember during copy editing is that you should check the material to see if it does break the law. If you think it does, change the words so that the problem is removed.

COPY FITTING

Now that each article has been edited, you know that it is publishable by your newsletter. However, your structure imposes space limitations and you need to be sure that all the material you have available will fit into the pages. This process is known as **copy fitting**.

How do I work it out?
Even if a contributor has written the number of words you require, the editing process thus far will have lengthened or shortened the original text. So now you must work out how many **column inches** the material will take up. This is simpler than it sounds. First, count the number of **characters** on five lines of a page. Divide this total by five to give you an average number of characters per line. Then multiply this total by the number of lines in the article. So your calculation for the total number of characters in the article is:

Total number of characters in five lines/5 x Total number of lines

For the next stage you will need to know how many characters of your chosen typeface you can fit in a single inch of one column of your particular design. All you need for this is some sample text in your chosen style. Measure three vertical inches of this text and count up the number of characters. Divide the answer by three to give you the average number of characters in a column inch.

To work out how much space a given article will take do the following calculation:

Number of characters in article/average number of characters per column inch

This will give you the number of inches of column space the article will take up. You can now work out how many column inches of material you have for each part of your newsletter structure. If any given section has more inches than can be fitted on the page you will need to cut out some material. If a section is not yet full, you will know how much more copy you need. If you cannot get more copy you should consider things like increasing the size of illustrations, or adding explanatory **subheadings**. It is rarely wise to add more words to the article as this will make it 'over-written'. If your copy editing work has been done properly the article you have in your hands will be the longest you should consider using.

PAGE LAYOUT

This is one of the last tasks in the editing process. Far too many newsletter producers start with this task. Indeed, you will re-member from our first case study that this was the basic mistake made by the estate agency. You can only do the page layout once all the articles have been copy edited, once copy fitting has been done and the illustrations selected. People using desktop publishing systems find it particularly hard to accept this. The DTP systems allow you to start your work with page layout. This is not a fault of the systems; they are merely tools to allow pages to be laid out, but it is the way DTP has come to be used. You can see many examples of shoddy work from desktop publishing systems. The vast majority of the errors are made because users start with page layout, rather than doing all the other very necessary work. Do not be tempted to rush into using your DTP system for your news-letter. You should only use the page layout tools at the end of the editorial process, not at the beginning.

Page layout is different to design. A designer will consider the look and feel of your publication and produce you overall guidelines on what is best suited to your needs. A page layout operator, on the other hand, takes your edited material and puts the jig-saw puzzle together so that it fits within the overall design specified by the designer. The essential elements of page layout are:

- positioning pictures
- positioning headlines
- positioning text
- positioning other items.

Positioning pictures

As you can see, pictures are listed at the top; these are the most important items on a page. They attract readers into your newsletter and so if they are put in the wrong place on the page it is easy for your readers to miss important material. The position of each picture will depend on its shape and to which item on a page it refers. However, it is always worth remembering that pictures on the top right quarter of a page attract most attention. Pictures at the bottom of a page receive least attention. If in any doubt as to where your pictures should go, put them on the top right of the page. (Many page layout artists would disagree and a number of the newsletters I produce do not follow this 'rule'. But if you are a beginner to page layout you will find this is an acceptable compromise until you are more confident with layout.)

Positioning headlines

The second most important items on a page are its headlines. Do not, unless you are an experienced layout artist, try fancy positions with headings. Put the headline at the top of the article. The most important headings should be larger and bolder than other headings on the same page. If you are not using typesetting, but depend on a typewriter, try using Letrast rub-down lettering for headings as this will look more attractive and will help readers.

Positioning the text

Text flows from left to right, from the top to the bottom. Basic, isn't it? But I remember a newspaper editor, who had no page layout experience, being a little dismayed when I pointed out to her that her layout wouldn't work because the first column of text was to the right of the second column. Just because you, as editor, know how the article flows does not mean your readers will automatically know. Wherever possible, important text should be near the top half of the page, with less important material lower down. Readers will expect vital information in the top of their newsletter, not sunk to the base of a page.

Positioning other items

There are many other bits and pieces that need to be placed in your pages. These include **boxes, rules, shaded panels** and the like. Use such items sparingly and position them with plenty of **white space** around them. Do not cram such items on a page.

The KISS principle

In all your page layout work please remember the KISS principle. This means:

Keep It Straight and Simple.

In other words do not make your layout complex or fussy. If it is simple and easy on the eye, your readers will find their way around quickly. If the layout is complex, readers will stumble and start disliking your newsletter because they find it hard to read.

HEADLINE WRITING

One of the items you position on the page layout is headline material. Headlines for your articles should always be written by the person doing the layout. Do not ask your contributors to come up with a heading. If they do provide you with one, ignore it. Headlines will be needed to fit specific slots of space, according to how the layout is done; headings provided by authors will rarely fit the space available. If you accept headings from writers you will need to adjust the layout and design to accommodate the words. This is bad practice because you will be losing the overall look and feel to some extent. Since this is fundamental to the success of your publication, if you accept headings from writers you will lose readers.

Instead, construct your headlines based on the space available and the design style which will say what typeface and typesize you need to use for each particular sort of heading. In Chapter 2 you will have seen the suggestion that headings can be in sans serif faces. But your basic design must incorporate more than this; there should be specific suggestions as to the size of the type you will use for headings. This must be adhered to, otherwise your newsletter will look different from one issue to the next and will therefore reduce reader loyalty.

What will attract readers?
In writing headlines you should realise that they are the key triggers to the emotions you are trying to target in your particular readers. So always use key words that set off those emotions in your headings. If, for instance, an emotion you need to trigger in your audience is one of sympathy, use headings like:

- Millchester family weep over lost dog
- Mother collapses in court hearing
- Couple in tears after bicycle burglary.

Headlines must be emotional triggers if they are to get your readers interested. Exploit those emotions and you will hook your readers. Ask yourself if readers would have read on if these example headings had been:

- Millchester family and their dog
- Mrs Wilson's court hearing
- The tale of two missing bicycles.

One other point about headings is to make them active. Far too many newsletters use passive headlines and so reduce reader interest. If the heading is active you will attract more readers. The first example headlines are active, while the second set are passive. Which interest you most?

PROOF READING

Even if you do not spend as much time as you should writing headings, or copy editing, do not under any circumstances neglect proof reading. One of the most glaring mistakes in any kind of publication is a spelling error. Your readers will laugh at you if your newsletter is constantly making mistakes. Check the pages of your newsletter thoroughly. Usually this means at least three

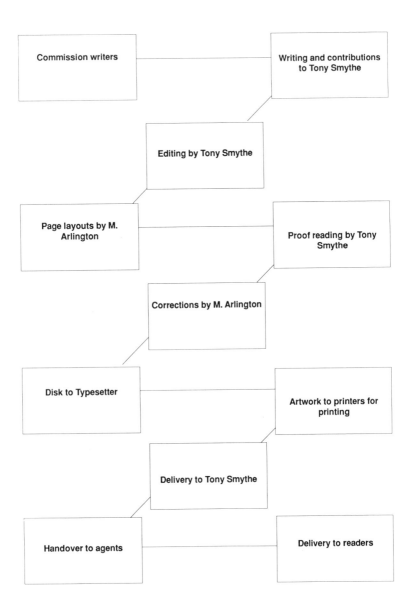

Fig. 4. An editorial process flow chart.

complete readings of each page, by two or three people who have not been involved in the writing or editing. If you have written or edited something you know what it should say, your brain will therefore interpret a spelling mistake as the correct word because you already know what should be there. Someone else, however, will read the word accurately and spot the mistake. If you do not have staff who can do this get your best mate, your wife, your husband, your mistress, your toyboy or your granny to do it. Anyone but you.

STONE SUBBING

This is the final stage of the production of your newsletter. The term comes from newspaper publishing, when the people who passed each page for printing worked with the print worker called a 'stone hand', who was the person who made up each page from the rows of metal type. Stone subbing still goes on in these computerised days. It is the task where someone checks each page to make sure that the stories fit the spaces allocated to them accurately. They also check that each story ends properly and that nothing is missing. Picture captions are checked to make sure they are with the right photograph and any embarrassing mistakes are finally ironed out.

Once you have proofread something there will inevitably be some mistakes which need sorting out. No matter whether you are using a typewriter or a typesetting machine, removing one mistake can generate another. Getting rid of such errors is the job of stone subbing. This task is your final check; it is the last job you do before sending your material away for printing, or agreeing to the photocopying. Do not neglect this job as it is vital to the effectiveness of your newsletter. A good idea is to get someone, anyone, to do this job who has not been involved at any previous stage. Glaring mistakes will then be picked up which you can correct before going to press.

GATHERING FEEDBACK

This is the final stage of the editing tasks which go to make up the editing process. Before you can continue with the next edition you need to be sure the last one is acceptable. In practical terms this may not always be possible; you may have started work on the second issue before the first one has even been printed. Nevertheless, the principle is one you should hold dear. Try to get feedback from your readers to find out what they think about your publication. You can do this with:

- a letters page
- competitions
- phone-in surveys
- reader questionnaires.

You could also enlist the services of a small group of readers who give you their comments on each issue, in return for a small fee. You can then use all the feedback you get to make alterations in any parts of the newsletter that are not as good as the audience expects then you start again on the editing process for the next issue.

The editorial process for your newsletter can be summarised as a flow chart. If you produce one similar to that in Figure 4, for the estate agency example, you will be on the right track.

Meeting the final copy deadline

5
Writing Your Newsletter

In the last chapter we saw how important it is to edit the copy you are provided with so that it is accurate, fair, consistent and according to your particular requirements. However, many newsletters do not have a great amount of outside contributions and the editor has to do all the writing. This chapter will help you write newsletter copy so that it is effective. The guidelines here also provide further details on how you can look at contributed copy and improve it.

THE *KISS* PRINCIPLE

If you missed it in Chapter 4, the KISS principle is:

Keep It Straight and Simple.

This applies not only to design but also to writing. One of the reasons I put you off using people who understand English to do your writing is that such individuals rarely follow the KISS principle. Lovers of the English language tend to use too many adjectives and skirt around an issue before making the point. In newsletter writing all you need to write is the point. No adjectives, no flowery language, no niceties; just straightforward, simple, communicative words.

THE *TELL* PRINCIPLE

The second principle of newsletter writing is TELL:

The Editor has Literary Licence.

In other words, if the editor doesn't like the way the words have been written they can be changed without need for the permission of the originator.

KISS and TELL

If you use KISS and TELL in your newsletter editing your text will be crisp, straight and easy to understand. However, far too many people do not use these principles, they accept what has been offered. Even if a newsletter editor does copy edit, he or she often feels loath to change the text too much. Do not be scared: change the words, alter the text. You know the newsletter far better than anyone else. You know the reader profile far better than anyone else. So you know, far better than anyone else, how things should be written.

Staff newsletters are a dead give-away of a lack of KISS and TELL. Usually, staff newsletters contain messages from the Chairman or important information from somebody in sales. Neither the Chairman nor the sales executive are trained writers, yet, newsletter editors fear changing their words. There is this fear in British industry which says you cannot change what a boss has written. Codswallop. You are the boss of the newsletter. The sales executive would change an advert, the Chairman would change a report for the board. So you can change the text for the newsletter. You will not lose your job for improving the image of your senior colleagues. You will lose your job if the newsletter fails as a result of a lack of readers because they couldn't wade their way through the dreadful writing of the Chairman!

Similarly, if you are editing a club newsletter, do not be frightened of altering the Secretary's report to make it more communicative. People will be glad of your improvements. Remember KISS and TELL.

STRAIGHT WRITING

If you have to write original material yourself, or re-write a colleague's words, you will need to keep the material straightforward. Exactly how you keep it that way depends very much on the subject matter. Keeping an article on the village cricket match straightforward is much easier than writing a discussion on the applications of the Fortran computer language in missile systems. Keeping your words straight is not the same as being simple, which we shall come to later in this chapter. Straight writing is communicative, understandable by the target audience and leads logically from one sentence to the next. Straight writing consists of the following features:

- good words
- short sentences
- understandable paragraphs
- structured outlines.

Words

These are the least of your problem. The words will flow naturally providing you have taken care of the structure of your article.

Sentences

Like words, these will naturally fall into place and will flow properly if your structured outline is right. However, one good tip about sentences is to have no more than 15 to 20 words in each. Sentences which are any longer have been shown by psychology reasearch to be difficult to understand. Sentences should also have few commas and other punctuation marks. Such marks are used to break up sentences to show pauses and the like. If you need to break up your sentences with commas and colons you should consider re-writing the text into two new sentences. One of the tests of the ease of reading of a document is to count the number of commas. A page of text is harder to read if it has a lot of commas.

Paragraphs

When you were at school you were probably taught to have paragraphs which contained a single concept. You were probably also told that the last sentence of a paragraph should lead you on towards the next. Well you can forget all that nonsense for newsletter writing. You need to break the habit of single concept paragraphs. In newsletters you will fare much better if each sentence is a single paragraph. Readership surveys have shown that this structure makes the columns easier to read because the paragraph breaks allow an optical illusion to occur. The small amount of white space at the start and end of each paragraph fools the reader into believing that there are fewer words on the page than actually printed. This causes a subconscious reaction suggesting that because there are fewer words, the article will be quick and easy to read. Without plenty of paragraph breaks, readers assume the text is longer than it is and are put off reading.

One other point about paragraphs. Take a look at anything you have written. Highlight the first and last sentence of each paragraph. Now read just the highlighted portions. In most cases the material will still make sense. This means your paragraphs are too long anyway as all the material in the middle of each paragraph is additional wordage which just gets in the way of the message. Try this test with material contributed to your newsletter to see how much you can cut out. Often there will be a great deal which can be dispensed with.

Outline
The essence of any good article will be its outline. Once you have produced your outline you will have a list of topics for each paragraph, which in most instances will provide you with the subject matter for each and every sentence of the article. If you use a computer-based word processor you should use the outlining feature, which most programs have. This will allow you to redefine the outline as your thoughts and ideas change.

An outline should be all your thoughts for a given article, just written down one at a time. Then group together the common themes and finally put all these themes in a logical order. You will then have a running order for each paragraph of your article. If you want to be sure that articles you commission from outside contributors follow your exact brief, then it is a good idea to produce the outline for the writer.

Example outline: Chapter 1
As an example of what an outline should look like, here is my structure for Chapter 1. This will help illustrate what an outline should look like. For most newsletter stories your outline will be shorter, but the principle is the same.

● Why publish newsletters?

● Age of information

    increase in leisure time

    changes in technology

reduced costs of production

- History of newsletters

    The Boston Newsletter

- Newsletter types

    News digests

    British Red Cross Society

    BLISS Newsletter

- Newsletter users

    Charities

    Churches

    Schools

    Friends

    Businesses

        staff newsletters

        Trebor

        NatWest

    Customer newsletters

    Marketing support newsletters

        Europrism

- Professions

    Doctors

Lawyers

Accountants

Binder Hamlyn

● Reasons for newsletters.

If you produce an outline of this nature for each article, no matter how small, the paragraphs automatically fall into place. This means the sentences also follow naturally and the words can virtually take care of themselves, at least as far as 'straight' writing is concerned.

SIMPLE WRITING

One thing about words which you should think about is their simplicity. Do not use complex words where more easily understood terms will do. Don't use technical terms where everyday words are easier to read and type. And never use 12 words where three will do. These are the most common writing mistakes in the choice of words.

Case history: The estate agent
Tony Smythe has written the first property news column for his newsletter. Below are his first few paragraphs:

'Standing in three acres of beautifully wooded hills, this 125 year old period cottage has just come onto our books and we believe it represents excellent value for money at just £275,000. This is a highly competitive pricing due in part to the owner's need to sell quickly due to the fact that he and his family are emigrating to Australia in the next three months, and also due to the fact that the garden is in need of some attention.

Inside the cottage you will find three well proportioned reception rooms, a fully fitted, fully tiled kitchen with Italian flooring and a downstairs cloakroom. Upstairs there are four bedrooms, one of which is en-suite with a fully tiled shower room, as well as a family bathroom. From the landing there are stairs to a study in the loft space.'

Tony thought this was rather good stuff and when he gave it to his local paper chum he was surprised when the material was completely re-written to read as follows:

'This period cottage in the woods is a real bargain. The owners are moving abroad and are keen to sell quickly. The price of the cottage is just £275,000.

Downstairs the cottage has three large rooms, one big enough for a snooker table. There is also a kitchen with Italian flooring.

Upstairs there are four bedrooms, two bathrooms and a study in the loft.

The garden is three acres but the grass does need cutting.'

The lessons learned

Tony's sentences were far too long. His paragraphs were too long as well. He used a number of words where one would do. He said, for example, 'well proportioned'. What's wrong with 'large'? Tony had also used estate agent jargon, like 'the garden is in need of some attention'. What's wrong with being more simplistic and saying 'the grass needs cutting'?

Write it as you would say it

When you are writing an article for your newsletter do not fall into the traps of this case study. Tony Smythe wrote it like he thought it should be written. He would not go up to his mate in the pub and say: 'This is a highly competitive pricing due in part to the owner's need to sell quickly due to the fact that he and his family are emigrating to Australia in the next three months, and also due to the fact that the garden is in need of some attention.'

He would say: 'This is a real bargain because the owners are going abroad. Mind you, the grass needs cutting as well so I've lopped a bit off the price for that.'

Estate agents aren't the only ones. Staff newsletters are full of gems. Bosses write things like:

'It is with the greatest of pleasure that the marketing department announce the formation of a new team of executives to target the ever growing sales opportunities in the teenage sector of the cosmetic marketplace.'

What's wrong with saying:

'Teenagers are being given special attention by a newly formed marketing team'?

Or what about:

'The ever increasing use of the XYS7543/874 washing machine has provided our research department with a real challenge in developing Wizzo, the new anti-olfactory, high-luminosity washing powder specifically designed for use in this microchip controlled machine.'

What would be wrong with:

'Developing Wizzo was a real challenge for our researchers. But they came up with a new powder that combats smells and makes whites brilliant. The powder is especially useful in Hotcity's new machine, the 'wondertub'.

Or what about:

'Our dramatic society's income has been rather poor of late thanks to the summer holidays and the additional effect of the formation of the operatic society which has eaten up some 27.56% of our funds in the third quarter of the year meaning we cannot afford the luxury of hired costumes for the pantomime.'

You could try:

'We probably won't be able to hire costumes for the panto, because our current funds are down by about a quarter. This is because many members have joined the operatic society.'

Just write things as you would say them in normal conversation and you won't go far wrong. However, don't use colloquialisms or swearwords or you will lose friends amongst your audience.

To keep your writing simple:

- use normal everyday words
- write it as you would say it
- avoid jargon
- don't use a number of words where fewer will do.

HOUSE STYLE

Whether you write the words or get them contributed, they must be within your normal style. If, say, you called the chairman by her first name in one article, but by her full title in another, your newsletter would not be consistent. You need to produce a written house style which should he adhered to. You should give your house style guide to all contributors and potential contributors so that material submitted is always to your rules.

House style contents
Your house style should contain the following main items:

- use of abbreviations
- use of accents
- use of capitals
- way in which proper nouns will be used
- use of diagrams
- use of numbers
- use of dates
- use of hyphens
- use of italics
- use of measurements
- style of references
- common spellings.

In this way, anyone writing an article which contains, say, proper nouns and some dates will be able to see how they should write them.

Your style may by 12/9/91 for dates, instead of 12th September 1991, or would you use September 12th, 1991, or perhaps 12 Sept 91?

Whichever style you settle upon, be consistent. If you do not provide a written guide to such items you will have a much harder time doing the copy editing as you will be constantly changing contributed text to fit within your house style.

A SAMPLE HOUSE STYLE

In order to show the detail with which you must produce your house style here is the style guide for the newsletters my organisation, ASPECT, publishes. You are free to use this style guide as your own, or as the basis of one which you develop.

House style
All publications produced by ASPECT adhere to the following style guidelines. If for any reason some part of the house style

needs altering this is discussed with each client at the outset of production.

Abbreviations and acronyms
Unless the abbreviation or acronym is familiar it will be spelt out in full on the first use in each article with the abbreviation or acronym in brackets immediately afterwards. Neither abbreviations nor acronyms will use any punctuation so there will not be any full points between characters. Only abbreviations listed in *Everyman's Dictionary of Abbreviations* will be acceptable.

Accents
Accents will only be used in words accepted as English when they make a difference to pronunciation or when they are used as proper nouns. At all other times no accents will be used.

Adjectives
The over-use of adjectives should be avoided.

Agreed
Things are agreed on or about and not simply agreed. 'Agreed to' will be avoided.

Americanisms
These should be avoided unless they are an integral part of the article.

Ampersands
Ampersands should only be used when they are part of a company or trade name.

Apostrophes
These will be used together with the letter 's' even after names which end in 's'. Thus Jones's is correct. Words will only end in an apostrophe when they are plurals.

Brackets
If an entire sentence is included within brackets the full stop is inside the brackets. Square brackets will be used for interpolation in directly quoted speech.

Capitals

The first word of each article will be in capitals. Words for capitalisation within sentences will be set in 'small caps' style. Initial capitals will only be used for proper nouns. Offices, titles of jobs and most government positions do not attract initial capitals. Organisations, company names and government departments do have initial capitals. Where there is any doubt about initial capitalisation lower case letters will be used. Trade names will have initial capitals only, the remainder of the word is lower case.

Collective nouns

A collective noun will be treated as singular. Therefore it is correct to say 'the company is preparing a statement', but wrong to say 'the company are preparing a statement'.

Colons

Colons should be avoided as they interrupt the flow of a sentence. However, a colon should always be used prior to a direct quote. (He said: 'This is the correct way to use a colon'.)

Commas

Commas should only be used where they are crucial to the understanding of a sentence. Clauses in mid sentence always require two commas—one before and one after the clause. In figures commas act as thousand separators.

Comparisons

Items which are compared to establish difference are compared 'with' and not 'to' one another. A is only compared to B when you wish to stress the similarity and not the difference.

Contractions

Contractions always attract a full point after them. Contractions can be distinguished from abbreviations since the last letter of the shortened form is the same as the last letter of the whole word, such as Road and Rd. This is not the case with an abbreviation. The exceptions to this rule are: Mr, Mrs, Ms, Dr, Revd, Mme and Mlle.

Countries

UK will be used in preference to England or Great Britain unless for specific reasons these are required. The United States of America will always be called US and not USA. Other countries will attract their full name.

Currencies
Pence or cents will be referred to as 3p or 6c, for instance. Whole pounds or dollars will be £4 or $3 without the following zeros. Millions will be referred to as 'm' such as £3m. Billions will be spelt out in full, as in £2 billion.

Dates
All dates will be as in 6th September 1992, ie number of day, month in full, year in full, with no commas.

Diagrams
All diagrams must be accompanied by an explanatory caption. Diagrams should be near the text which refers to them. Where diagrams are numbered they will be referred to as 'Figure 1' and so on.

Equations and formulae
Any mathematical equations or formulae should use the appropriate typographical markings. Any confusions should be cleared by referring to *Hart's Rules for Compositors and Typesetters*.

Figures
Sentences should not begin with figures. Preferably they should be re-written so that the sentence begins with another word. Alternatively the figures should be spelt out as words. Fractions will not be used and should be converted to decimals. All numbers from one to ten will be spelt out in full. From 11 upwards figures will be used. The % sign will be used rather than the words per cent.

Former
The words former and latter will not be used as they are potentially confusing.

Full stops
These are not used in headings or sub-headings. Full stops are not used in abbreviations, acronyms or certain contractions.

Hyphens

These should be avoided as they disrupt reading. Most words that begin with 'anti' and 'non' will have hyphens. Adjectives formed from more than two words will also have hyphens. Ambiguities can be avoided by the use of hyphens. If entire sections of copy are justified, hyphenation will be used and hyphens will be placed in the appropriate position as defined by the Proximity/Merriam Webster Linguabase hyphenation dictionary.

Initials

Initials in proper names should be avoided and forenames spelt in full. If initials must be used they should be followed by a full point.

Inverted commas

Directly quoted speech is contained within single inverted commas. Double quotation marks should only be used for quotations within speech. Punctuation always remains within inverted commas. Full points at the end of directly quoted speech come after the last word and prior to the inverted comma. The exception to this rule is where the quotation does not form the entire sentence.

Italics

Italics should be avoided as they are difficult to read. They should only be used for the names of publications, for foreign words and for the names of species.

Jargon

This should be avoided completely.

Lists

Each item to be listed should be placed on a separate line. Lists should not be made of items following a colon and separated with semi-colons.

Measures

When possible all measurements will be in metric units. All units will be abbreviated in lower case without full points. There will be no space between the figure and the unit. Thus 5cm and 6km are correct. Squares and cubes will be referred to with a superscript 2 or 3.

Metaphors
These should be avoided.

Names
Full names and title will be used in the first instance but afterwards merely title and surname will be used. Thus the first mention would be Mr Bill Bloggs and thereafter all mentions would be Mr Bloggs.

References
Bibliographical references shall follow the guidelines laid down by the Cambridge University Press for non-scientific works. For scientific works the guidelines of the Council for Biology Editors will be used. Journal references shall be as follows: Name of author Title of paper Name of Journal Volume number: page range; year of publication. Punctuation shall be as shown here. Therefore only one colon, one semi colon and one full point are required. There are no commas used and all type is set in Roman style without emboldening or italicisation.

Semi-colons
These are used to mark a pause longer than a comma, but shorter than a full point. In general semi-colons should be avoided as they interrupt reading.

Sentences
These should be short and crisp. An average sentence length of 15 words is the most acceptable.

Short words
Use as many of these as possible as they aid reading. Long words confuse and make the publication less successful.

Slang
Avoid this completely unless used to make a point.

Spellings
The spellings used are established English spellings checked in both *Chambers Dictionary* and the *Oxford English Dictionary*. Important spellings to note are shown below:

Aging
Burnt
Disk
Focused
Fulfil
Grey
Hiccough
Hello
Judgment
Licence (noun)
License (verb)
Mileage
Paediatric
Practice (noun)
Practise (verb)
Program (computers only)
Realise
Swap (not swop)
Telephone (not phone)
Withhold

Time
Time will be in the 12-hour clock with 'am' or 'pm' appearing immediately after the time with no space and no punctuation.

Unnecessary words
Much copy contains extra words which add nothing to the meaning and only serve to confuse. These should be avoided and should be removed where appropriate.

A TRUE STORY

A couple of years ago I produced a newsletter for a pharmaceutical company. I forgot to hand them my style guide. When the first page proofs were prepared I used my usual stylistic rules. This meant a number of changes to the copy and particularly changes to the references as these had been prepared in another style altogether.

The first page proofs were rejected because of the style changes I had made. I then realised I had not provided the style guide and had forgotten to make it clear that all the publications ASPECT produces adhere to a common house style. The pharmaceutical company did not have its own house style. It was merely concerned with the fact that I had changed the style of the text, particularly the references. After some discussion the company insisted I change everything back to the way the contributors had prepared their text. Naturally, this meant additional work which I had not budgeted for. Meanwhile I sent my style guide to the company. Then came the telephone call. They hadn't realised that my style was based on accepted publishing practice, they thought I was just making things up to suit me! So, could I change everything back to my style! Again, more work and as you can probably guess, I've never forgotten to hand over the style guide again.

The lessons learned
If you do not give your style guide to your contributors you will find yourself doing more work than necessary. Everyone who could contribute to your newsletter should be handed a printed style guide. If you can't develop one of your own, use mine shown above.

INDIVIDUALITY

Although you should ensure that your newsletter has consistent style, this does not mean you should limit the individuality of writers. In just the same way as we all speak or walk differently, so we all write in various ways. Although you should insist that people stick to your house style, don't be so rigid that they cannot write in their own way. If you impose too rigid a house style you will stop good expression from writers and your newsletter will be very boring to read. A variety of styles is good for your publication as it will stimulate the interest of your audience.

To encourage individuality from your writers just tell them to sit at their typewriter or word processor and write. As long as they have an outline for their article and they don't worry about the words, the sentences will flow fairly naturally. If you can encourage people to write just as they speak, their individuality will be expressed.

If you are writing most of the newsletter yourself do not worry about trying to express a variety of styles. Stick to being natural. Even though your readers would like a bit of variation, your newsletter will be much more successful if you do not make forlorn attempts to vary your writing style.

THE FINAL ANALYSIS

Whether you write your newsletter or you get material from outside contributors you only need to remember two things:

KISS and TELL.

● Keep It Straight and Simple.

● The Editor has Literary Licence.

How to Write for Publication

Chriss McCallum

'Handy for both professional and newcomer alike.' *Writers News*. 'Everything you ever wanted to know about the practical side of publishing . . . excellent.' *Competitors Journal*. 'Really definitive—a book that seems to have every possible question answered in a straightforward, concise and clear manner . . . Leaves every other similar book in its shade.' *Pause (National Poetry Foundation)*. 'It is, quite simply, one of the best books of its kind that I've ever read.' Steve Wetton, Author of BBC TV's comedy drama *Growing Pains*. 'The revised and updated second edition maintains the high standard . . . Its reference section of useful addresses is value for money on its own.' *Writers News*.

£8.99, 192 pp illus. 1 85703 140 7. 3rd edition.

Please add postage & packing (UK £1 per copy, Europe £2 per copy, World £3 per copy, airmail).

How To Books Ltd, Plymbridge House, Estover Road, Plymouth PL6 7PZ, United Kingdom. Tel: (01752) 695745. Fax: (01752) 695699. Telex: 45635.

Credit card orders may be faxed or phoned.

6
Using Illustrations in Newsletters

WHAT ARE THE BENEFITS?

Wherever possible you should add illustrations to your newsletter. Pictures of all kinds bring your newsletter alive and make it appear more interesting. Reading research shows that the first item we look at on a page is the illustration. If there is no picture on a page the interest level of readers is much lower and their attention span is reduced. In other words, without pictures on your pages you will not get as many readers as you could.

Many newsletters do include pictures, but large numbers do not have them. This is not a budgetary consideration, but a false assumption. The editors seem to think that if they are producing serious, intelligent, academic type newsletters their readers will not expect illustrations. The result is that the readers see the publications as dry, serious and rather uninteresting. Such newsletters could dramatically increase their readership levels by including pictures.

Increasing your readership is not the only benefit of pictures. Psychological research has shown that where there are pictures on a page readers understand the articles more easily and remember them more readily. In other words, with pictures on a page you are being more communicative. You are succeeding in getting a message across to your readers. The reason for this additional benefit of pictures is thanks to an optical illusion. Where there are pictures there has to be less text on the page. Because there is less text readers subconsciously assume that the shorter articles must therefore be easier to read. They approach the page with a more open and ready mind. If there is no illustration, the extent of the text appears daunting and readers approach the page with some trepidation. They think they ought to read it but are concerned at the volume of text they will have to consume. The result is they are less interested, more easily distracted and so take in less.

If you use pictures in your newsletter you will:

- attract more readers
- retain their attention longer
- enable them to understand more
- allow them to remember more of the text.

The result is that pictures allow you to communicate.

TYPES OF ILLUSTRATIONS

There is a variety of illustrations you can use for your newsletter and if possible you should vary the ones you use to provide increased interest and novelty. The types you should consider are:

- photographs
- maps
- diagrams
- charts
- tables
- drawings
- cartoons.

CHOOSING ILLUSTRATIONS

The type of illustration you use in your newsletter will depend on your budgets, your printing process and the reader expectation. There are some key things to remember when selecting illustrations for your newsletter. No matter what kind of illustration you are using it must have the following assets:

- relevance
- interest
- composition
- balance
- tone
- good physical characteristics.

Relevance
It may seem facile, but make sure your picture is relevant to the

story it is due to accompany. I have seen countless newsletter pages where the picture next to a story seems strange. The reason was that the picture was not strictly relevant to the story. Say you have to illustrate the chief executive's lecture on the company's future. You could put a picture of the boss delivering his talk. That's just about acceptable, but boring and not 'relevant' to the readers. They already know what the boss looks like.

More relevant would be a picture showing the plans for the new building programme, or a chart showing expected increases in turnover, or a picture of all the extra staff employed in the last year showing how good things must be. Relevance is about what is most likely to interest your readers, so choose a picture that will fit your psychological profile, rather than just anything which could accompany a story.

Interest

This is not the same as relevance. You may have chosen a relevant picture, but is it interesting? Does it strike you and make you sit up and look at it? A picture of all the new employees at your factory may be relevant, but is it an interesting shot? A map showing the way to your new tennis club may be relevant, but is the illustration striking? If not, choose an alternative. What you are looking for in a relevant picture is something which will grab your readers' attention. If the picture strikes you instantly, use it, because it is almost certainly going to do the same to your readers.

Composition

This is partly about the rule of thirds, mentioned in Chapter 4. If your picture is relevant and interesting it must also be composed properly. In other words has the photographer or artist produced an image which looks attractive? If all the people are bunched up in a corner, or if the focal point of a map is squeezed down one side, the composition is wrong. The pictures in Figures 5 and 6 show the difference between good and poor composition.

Balance

Providing the illustration has met all the other criteria, you need to make sure it is balanced. The picture may be composed properly and used the rule of thirds, but has too much attention been given to one item or person? If the picture is about new employees, for example, have you accurately represented the proportions of young and old, male and female? In looking at the balance of the picture you are essentially trying to establish whether it is a fair representation of the truth.

Tone

The final aspect of choosing an illustration is its tone. If you are looking at a photograph you will need to make sure it is not too dark or too light. Is there a good spread of greys or colours? Similarly when looking at a drawing you will need to make sure that the picture is not lacking in variation and contrast. Check that there is a good spread of colour or shading. If you are producing a chart, for instance, have you used a sufficient variety of shades or colours to help readers distinguish relevant factors? What you are looking for in the tone of any illustration is a spread of colours and greys that makes it easier for readers to appreciate the illustration.

Physical characteristics

Photographs

You have two choices with photographs, black and white or colour. Whichever you wish to use you should make sure that you have the cleanest, crispest shot available.

Black and white photographs
Make sure the picture is clearly in focus. Many publications reduce their impact by using poorly focused pictures.

Choose a glossy print if possible. These are brighter and reproduce better than those printed matt.

Choose a print that is a standard 10 x 8 as this allows better reproduction.

Colour photographs
Wherever possible use colour slides as you will get a much better reproduction from these. You will also get a better image if you use medium format slides which are 5cm x 5cm. Other medium format sizes are also acceptable. If 35mm slides are all that are available then these are usable, but will give less brilliant reproduction than larger sizes.

If you must use colour prints use 7 x 5 size. This will give a good reproduction without looking too grainy and without affecting the colours.

Fig. 5.   Good composition . . .

Fig. 6.   . . . and poor.

When selecting colour pictures make sure they are in focus and that there is a good colour balance. Do not accept a picture if it looks as though it has a predominance of one colour. This will be worsened in the reproduction process. To select colour slides you should either project them on to a clear white screen, or use a light box. These boxes can be obtained from high street photography stores. Do not select colour slides by holding them to your eye and squinting at them towards a window or light bulb. You will not see the picture clearly and could choose one which will not reproduce adequately.

Maps

Many maps for newsletters will be drawn specifically to accompany a particular article. The maps should preferably be on stiff white card and should be no larger than A4. The lines should be drawn with a proper drawing pen, obtained from artists' supplies shops or stationers. Do not use felt tips or roller ball pens as the lines will not be accurate and reproduction will not be as good as if you use proper pens.

If a map is in colour you will find that traditional mapping colours are difficult to reproduce. Indeed, the variety of fine colours used in many maps is used specifically to stop counterfeiting and colour photocopying. If you intend using a colour map ensure the colours are bright.

Diagrams, charts, tables, drawings

What has been said for maps also applies to diagrams, charts, tables and drawings. The illustrator should use good pens and apply colour appropriately. Many of these illustrations can be drawn on computer. If you are using a computer to produce any kind of diagram or illustration draw it at the size you want in the newsletter, or slightly larger. If you draw it smaller, the increase in size could affect the quality of reproduction. Similarly, if you draw it too large, the final illustration may be difficult to understand as it has to be crammed into a smaller space. In fact, this is a good tip for all illustrations, whether they are produced on a computer or traditionally. You will get much better results if the actual illustration is the same size as it will appear in the newsletter.

Cartoons

Most cartoons you use will be drawn by professional cartoonists who know how to prepare their work. In general, cartoons should be on stiff card and prepared on high white paper background to aid reproduction. All of the characteristics of charts and diagrams also apply to cartoons.

SOURCES OF ILLUSTRATIONS

So now you know what to choose, but where do you get your illustrations from? There is a wide variety of sources and the one you choose will depend upon your financial plans and the reader profile. Essentially the available sources break down to the following categories:

● yourself
● amateur freelancers
● professional freelancers
● photographic libraries
● photo agencies
● public relations companies
● business and industry.

Doing the illustrations yourself

No matter what type of newsletter you are producing, do not neglect yourself as a provider of illustrations. After all, you are the only person who has read and edited all the text so you are the one individual who knows exactly what kind of illustration is required. Why put Chinese whispers to the test and get an unusable picture, when you know just what is required? However, do not try producing your own illustrations unless you can:

● take good photographs
● or draw to high standards.

If you need help in either you could go to evening classes, or take a correspondence course. Rapid Results College (tel: 0181-947 7272) for instance, does a City & Guilds course in photography. The British Association of Communicators in Business also does a course called 'Editor as Photographer'.

If you do decide to provide your own illustrations you must use the tests of choosing a picture as described earlier in this chapter.

Do not simply use any picture you produce just because you did it!

Using amateur freelancers

If you are producing a newsletter for your club or association you will have a veritable supply of such individuals. If you are working on a staff newsletter you will have plenty of volunteers for taking pictures. Even if you are producing a business newsletter for your customers you will find that eager members of your staff suggest they could take the pictures. While it is all very good to have such a plethora of volunteers, do not accept the invitations with readiness. Use the rules on selecting contributors given in Chapter 4.

If you do find that friends and colleagues are able to provide the sort of material you want, be sure to brief them exactly so that they give you the physical characteristics you need. Your chum in the netball club may be a good photographer, but if she provides you with 35mm slides, when you really wanted 10 x 8 prints, you will be forced into extra expense and will sacrifice quality of reproduction. To help you get the best out of amateur freelancers use the checklist for a requisition form below.

Request for illustration:

Type of illustration required
(photograph/drawing/map/chart/cartoon):   _____
Deadline for delivery: _____
Details of illustration: _____
Colours: black and white/two colours/full colour: _____
Physical characteristics: _____
Copyright details: _____
Fee: _____

If you fill in the details on this form you will be in a much better position. You will have given precise instructions to your friend or colleague, so you should get exactly what you want. If the amateur illustrator provides something else you can legitimately say that it isn't suitable because your instructions haven't been followed.

Using professional freelancers
Details of where to find professional freelancers were given in
Chapter 4. If possible ask to see samples of their work so you can
be sure the illustrator produces the kind of material you want. All
professional freelancers will be happy to send you copies of their
published work or to visit you and show you a portfolio. When
you commission material from a freelance professional you should
issue an official order. You could use the same form as for amateur
freelancers, if you wanted.

Using photographic libraries
There are many libraries of photographs and you can use pictures
stocked by these companies in your newsletter. A large number of
libraries are general and provide pictures on all sorts of topics.
However, there are plenty of specialist libraries which provide
pictures on specific topics. There is a wildlife library, for instance,
a botanic library, a science library and an aerial views library.

All photo libraries publish catalogues of their work. Each of the
pictures is shown in miniature together with a reference number.
You can obtain the catalogues by calling the libraries and asking
for one; the catalogues are free. You can get the numbers of photo
libraries from *Creative Review* magazine, from large newsagents,
or from the *Writers' and Artists' Yearbook*.

To order from a photo library all you do is call and quote the
reference number. You will then be asked a series of questions
such as:

- What size will the printed picture be?
- What type of publication will it appear in?
- What is the circulation of your publication?
- Will it be on the front cover or inside?
- What country will the publication circulate in?

You will then be given a price for the use of the photograph. If
you accept the quoted fee you will be sent the picture and a
contract. You sign the contract and return the photograph once
you have used it. The contract will say exactly what use the picture
is for. Library contracts also make it clear that you cannot duplicate
the picture and that you are only renting it for the specific use
detailed.

The price of library pictures varies enormously. The fee depends on the size, the number of readers you have, whether it is a cover shot and who took the photograph. Libraries include shots from relatively unknown photographers to international stars of photography. Clearly you will be charged more for a David Bailey than you would for a Graham Jones picture!

As a guide you could expect to pay around £100 for a little known photographer in a newsletter that went to around 4,000 people. For a better known photographer on the cover of the same sort of newsletter you could expect to pay around £350.

Using photo agencies
Photographic agencies are similar to libraries, except that these companies employ their own photographers. Agencies can also respond to news items and will syndicate pictures widely amongst newspapers and magazines. The process for ordering pictures from agencies is much the same as for libraries. Again you can find the names of photo agencies in *Creative Review* or the *Writers' and Artists' Yearbook*.

Using public relations companies
PR agencies will also provide photographs. In most instances you can ignore them. Usually the pictures they provide do not match the tests of a good picture outlined earlier in this chapter. They generally lack relevance and interest, although technically the photographs from public relations companies are very good.

If, however, you cannot afford your own photographs, public relations agencies are worth contacting. They will often provide a reasonable photograph or even set one up for you for nothing, in return for some publicity for their client. However, be sure to state exactly what you want in any picture and the physical format you require.

Approaching business and industry
There is a vast untapped resource of illustrations in every company in the UK. All businesses have illustrations of some kind and are generally willing for newsletter editors to borrow them as this produces 'free' publicity. If you are producing a newsletter for your local fishing club and want to write about the new rod you have been using, why not call the manufacturers and ask for some pictures? The company will almost certainly have the illustrations and you will get them for nothing.

If you are producing a staff newsletter and are writing about the new extension being built to the factory, you can be sure the architect has some designs or a model that could be used for illustrations, rather than your picture of the hole in the ground.

When using other businesses for pictures, be clear to state exactly what you want and the format you require. Also give them a deadline. If you just ask them to send the picture as soon as possible you will never get it.

USING ILLUSTRATIONS

So you have now chosen the right source for your pictures and selected the ones you want to use. The effectiveness of the final printed image is now up to you. Although Chapter 4 made it clear that pictures are better in the top half of your page, there is more to using images than just sticking them in the best position. In the same way that Chapter 5 explained copy editing, the remainder of this chapter will now take you through picture editing.

There are four main elements to picture editing. These are:

- scaling
- cropping
- retouching
- reversing.

Scaling pictures

Although you may produce diagrams and charts to the right size, often you will not know how much space you have for an illustration at the time you commission it. Also, black and white pictures will invariably be larger than you need and colour pictures will be smaller. To get the picture to the size you need it in your newsletter you will need to scale it. This means adjusting the width in proportion to the height. If you increase the width by 25%, then the height must also be raised by the same amount to avoid distortion. Exactly how you go about scaling an illustration will depend upon the production method you use. If you are using computers the programs can scale pictures automatically for you, so you avoid the calculations. However, if you are using traditional reproduction methods you will need to scale an illustration using the following technique:

1. Stick a piece of tracing paper to the back of the picture and fold it over so that it covers the entire front of the illustration.

2. Draw a line, using a soft pencil, to mark the edges of the picture.

3. Draw another line to connect the bottom left corner with the top right corner.

4. Now mark a point along the bottom line to represent the exact width you want the printed picture to be.

5. Draw a line from this point vertically to the diagonal line.

6. Now draw a line from where this new line connects to the diagonal horizontally to the left edge.

7. The tracing paper should now look like that in Figure 7.

Essentially you have drawn two boxes. One, the larger, represents the full size of the image. The smaller box shows the size it will appear in your newsletter. Of course, you can do the reverse with a larger sheet of tracing paper. You simply extend the diagonal line and then mark the width you want the picture to be.

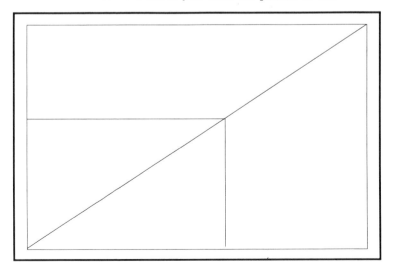

Fig. 7.   How to scale drawings up or down.

In any event, the distance between the diagonal line and the mark representing your required width is the height the scaled image will take up on the printed page.

Cropping pictures

In many instances the pictures you obtain will fit all of your criteria for usage, except that there will be additional material in the photograph you would rather wasn't printed. To get rid of this material you employ cropping. This is a simple matter of removing what you do not want. You do not have to cut the picture, you simply draw your first lines on the tracing paper overlay to surround the area of the picture you do want to use, before doing the scaling. If you are using a commercial printing company they will exclude the area you don't want used before processing the picture. If you are using a computer, cropping can be done easily by masking out the areas you don't want printed.

Fig. 8.   Cropping one photograph, to produce several illustrations.

Cropping is also a useful way of getting more than one illustration from a single picture. Look at the example in Figure 8 and you will see that three different illustrations have been produced from just one picture by the effective use of cropping.

Retouching pictures

Sometimes cropping is not enough to get rid of the part of a picture you want excluded. This is where retouching comes into play. The original photograph is **scanned** into a sophisticated computerised machine. Once the scan is made the original is no longer required and remains unaltered. However, the scanned copy can be completely changed. Say, for instance, the only available picture of your office block has an unsightly black cloud in the background. Don't worry, retouching can remove the offending cloud. What if the only picture of your boss shows a cigarette in her hand and she has now given up smoking? Never mind, retouching can remove the cigarette and get rid of the puff of smoke. Essentially retouching can do whatever you want. You can even combine photographs with retouching techniques. Say your squash club newsletter wants to show a picture of the new president, but the only picture you have is of the new chap at his old club! Well you simply use retouching to remove the image of the president and place him in a picture of your club. The join is invisible.

Of course, there is a price to pay for retouching techniques. It is vastly expensive and you will need to budget around £500 for even the most basic work. However, new programs are now available for desktop publishing systems and a number of bureaux are setting up around the country to take advantage of them. What this means is that you will be able to get retouching done at a fraction of the price, perhaps for around £30 per picture. Most of the bureaux who offer this new work advertise in *Mac User* magazine, available from newsagents.

Reversing pictures

One final aspect of picture editing is reversing. Generally, if there are people in your pictures you want to position them so that they are looking towards the middle of your newsletter and towards the appropriate article. This is not always possible because your newsletter structure is going to impose some limits. The way out of this is to reverse the picture. Desktop publishing systems can do this and anyone using traditional printing just asks the typesetting firm to reverse the picture. What happens is that the person looking to the right is now facing left and vice versa.

However, there are potential problems with reversing pictures. If there are any letters or signs in the picture these will be reversed and look like Russian! If the individual has recognisable marks, they will now appear on the other side of their body, and if the person in the photograph is married, their wedding ring will have miraculously jumped to their right hand. (That can also be potentially libellous, so beware.) If you must reverse a picture look at it with great care beforehand and if necessary crop out any giveaways that show the image has been turned round.

HANDLING ILLUSTRATIONS

The final thing you should be aware of in using illustrations is how to handle them. Basically this boils down to 'handle with care'.

- Do not touch the illustrations themselves, always handle the edges only.

- Keep your illustrations in plastic covers.

- Store your illustrations vertically. Do not pile them up as this will damage them.

- Keep your illustrations out of sunlight and store them away from sources of heat like radiators.

If you look after your illustrations you will soon have your own library and could even earn income for your newsletter by renting out pictures to other publishers!

POINTS TO THINK ABOUT

1. How important would illustrations be in your own newsletter?
2. What kind of illustration sources would you turn to?
3. What budget do you have for illustrations in each issue?
4. What would be the main problems to be overcome for you in illustrating a newsletter? How could you tackle them?

7
Putting Your Newsletter Together

Earlier in this book the various methods of production were touched upon. You can use traditional techniques, computers or rely on a typewriter. This chapter will take you forward from your edited copy, your scaled and cropped pictures and allow you to put your pages together, physically. Do not attempt to put your newsletter together unless you have completed all the stages outlined in Chapters 4, 5 and 6.

GETTING STARTED

To start the physical production of your newsletter you will need the following items:

- properly edited copy
- scaled and cropped illustrations
- a ruler
- a soft pencil
- a red pen
- blank white paper the same size as your newsletter pages
- paper glue
- paper clips
- stapler.

(Some of these items, such as glue and a stapler, are not necessary if you are using a computer. But you will need the other items.)

GRIDS

The essential starting point of the production of any publication is a grid. This is a basic tool which shows the number and width of the columns on a page. The grid also has a number of horizontal

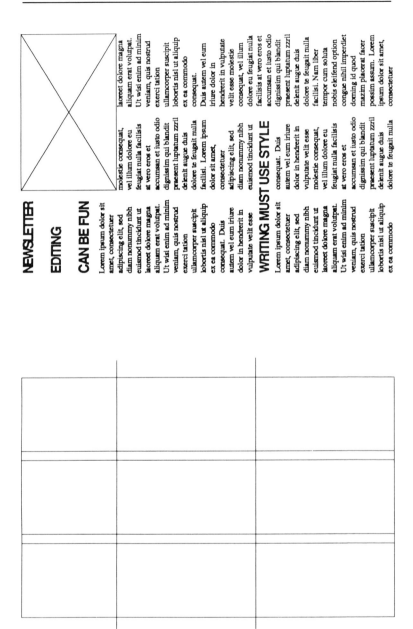

Fig. 9. A three-column page grid system, divided horizontally into thirds.

NEWSLETTER EDITING

CAN BE FUN

Lorem ipsum dolor sit amet, consectetuer adipiscing elit, sed diam nonummy nibh euismod tincidunt ut laoreet dolore magna aliquam erat volutpat. Ut wisi enim ad minim veniam, quis nostrud exerci tation ullamcorper suscipit lobortis nisl ut aliquip ex ea commodo consequat. Duis autem vel eum iriure dolor in hendrerit in vulputate velit esse molestie consequat, vel illum dolore eu feugiat nulla facilisis

at vero eros et accumsan et iusto odio dignissim qui blandit praesent luptatum zzril delenit augue duis dolore te feugait nulla facilisi. Lorem ipsum dolor sit amet, consectetuer adipiscing elit, sed diam nonummy nibh euismod tincidunt ut laoreet dolore magna aliquam erat volutpat. Ut wisi enim ad minim veniam, quis nostrud exerci tation ullamcorper suscipit lobortis nisl ut aliquip ex ea commodo consequat.

SUBHEAD

Duis autem vel eum iriure dolor in hendrerit in vulputate velit esse molestie consequat, vel illum dolore eu feugiat nulla facilisis at vero eros et accumsan et iusto odio dignissim qui blandit praesent luptatum zzril delenit augue duis dolore te feugait nulla facilisi. Nam liber

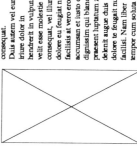

WRITING MUST USE STYLE

Lorem ipsum dolor sit amet, consectetuer adipiscing elit, sed diam nonummy nibh euismod tincidunt ut laoreet dolore magna aliquam erat volutpat. Ut wisi enim ad minim veniam, quis nostrud exerci tation ullamcorper suscipit lobortis nisl ut aliquip ex ea commodo consequat. Duis autem vel eum iriure dolor in hendrerit in vulputate velit esse molestie consequat, vel illum dolore eu feugiat nulla facilisis at vero eros et accumsan et iusto odio dignissim qui blandit praesent luptatum zzril

---

NEWSLETTER EDITING

CAN BE FUN

Lorem ipsum dolor sit amet, consectetuer adipiscing elit, sed diam nonummy nibh euismod tincidunt ut laoreet dolore magna aliquam erat volutpat. Ut wisi enim ad minim veniam, quis nostrud exerci tation ullamcorper suscipit lobortis nisl ut aliquip ex ea commodo consequat. Duis autem vel eum iriure dolor in hendrerit in vulputate velit esse molestie consequat, vel illum dolore eu feugiat nulla facilisis

at vero eros et accumsan et iusto odio dignissim qui blandit praesent luptatum zzril delenit augue duis dolore te feugait nulla facilisi. Lorem ipsum dolor sit amet, consectetuer adipiscing elit, sed diam nonummy nibh euismod tincidunt ut laoreet dolore magna aliquam erat volutpat. Ut wisi enim ad minim veniam, quis nostrud exerci tation ullamcorper suscipit lobortis nisl ut aliquip ex ea commodo consequat.

SUBHEAD

at vero eros et accumsan et iusto odio dignissim qui blandit praesent luptatum zzril delenit augue duis dolore te feugait nulla facilisi. Lorem ipsum dolor sit amet, consectetuer adipiscing elit, sed diam nonummy nibh euismod tincidunt ut laoreet dolore magna aliquam erat volutpat. Ut wisi enim ad minim veniam, quis nostrud exerci tation ullamcorper suscipit lobortis nisl ut aliquip ex ea commodo consequat.

Duis autem vel eum iriure dolor in hendrerit in vulputate velit esse molestie consequat, vel illum dolore eu feugiat nulla facilisis at vero eros et accumsan et iusto odio dignissim qui blandit praesent luptatum zzril delenit augue duis dolore te feugait nulla facilisi. Nam liber tempor cum soluta

WRITING MUST USE STYLE

Lorem ipsum dolor sit amet, consectetuer adipiscing elit, sed diam nonummy nibh euismod tincidunt ut laoreet dolore magna aliquam erat volutpat. Ut wisi enim ad minim veniam, quis nostrud exerci tation ullamcorper suscipit lobortis nisl ut aliquip ex ea commodo consequat. Duis autem vel eum iriure dolor in hendrerit in vulputate velit esse molestie consequat, vel illum dolore eu feugiat nulla facilisis

SUBHEAD

at vero eros et accumsan et iusto odio dignissim qui blandit praesent luptatum zzril delenit augue duis dolore te feugait nulla facilisi. Lorem ipsum dolor sit amet, consectetuer adipiscing elit, sed diam nonummy nibh euismod tincidunt ut laoreet dolore magna facilisi. Lorem ipsum dolor sit amet,

lines across the columns to break the page up into portions. The number and size of the portions is entirely up to you.

The lines of your grid are used to line things up. If you do not use a grid your layouts will not have an underlying structure. Just as your entire newsletter must have a basic structure, so must your design. A good structure to a page grid system means that readers will automatically know where to look next on a page. The grid acts as a kind of invisible signposting system.

In Figure 9 you will see a three-column page which has been divided into thirds horizontally. The figure also shows three pages based on the grid system, which all look different but have a coherency and consistency forced upon them by the grid. Take a look at your favourite magazine and look at the position of items on various pages. You should begin to see the publication's grid emerge.

If you are using a computer you can set up grids automatically in most programs. If you are not using a computer you should draw your grid accurately on paper and then use copies of this master page as the basis for producing each separate page of your newsletter.

How do I use grids?

Pictures
To start your production work you will need a clean grid. Now take your soft pencil and draw on the grid the position of the illustrations. The drawing should be accurate and you should use your ruler to get the right dimensions. Then draw two lines connecting the opposite corners of the picture box so that you have a cross in the centre, as shown in Figure 10. This is the standard way of indicating the **position of the picture** on the page. Now write inside the box a reference number for the picture. Usually, pictures are referred to alphabetically. So if this is the first picture in the issue just write 'A' in the box. Next, on the tracing paper overlay on the picture also write 'A'. Now you and your printer know exactly what picture should go where.

Headlines
The next task is to indicate on your grid where the headlines will go. The basic design you produced when reading Chapter 4 should have roughly shown this, now you must be more accurate. Write

in the headline on the grid with the red pen at roughly the size it will appear in print. Make sure you use just the same amount of space as you want the headline to take up.

Articles
Now measure from the bottom of the headline down the column the number of inches the particular article will take up. You should

Fig. 10.   How to indicate a picture position on a page.

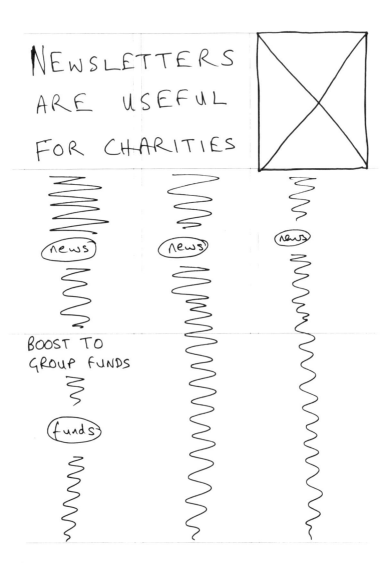

Fig. 11.   The final stage of using a grid.

have calculated this measurement in the copy fitting stage of editing. Use the soft pencil to shade in the area which the text will fill. Now with the red pen write over the shading the name of the article.

Repeat this exercise for each item on your page. Your grid should now look like the example in Figure 11.

Using a grid really helps

That is all there is to using the grid. The vertical and horizontal lines on the page are there simply to help you produce your layout accurately. During the editing process you will have a rough idea of how each page will look. But it is only in this production stage, when you use your grid to align items properly, that you get your first view of what the page will look like.

If you use a computer I suggest you do this manual work as well. This may seem unnecessary extra work, but it is an excellent aid to your production task. If you ignore this stage you can still produce your pages, but you will spend more time than necessary. The reason is that you will need to keep redesigning the page on the computer screen until things fit properly. This takes more time than working it out by hand on a grid sheet. If you use computers, you should still rely on this older technology as it will save you time. You will also find it easier to produce your pages.

To start the production of your newsletter all you need do is prepare a basic, but accurate, drawing for each page on your grid sheets. In Chapter 4 the basics of page design were outlined. There are many good books on page design and there is not sufficient space in this book to provide further detail. (See Further Information for specific book titles.)

MARKING UP

Now that your grids are prepared you should attach all of the articles and all of the pictures that are relevant to each page to the grid. Clip the items together so that everything associated with a single page is in one place. You will also need to write each headline on a separate piece of blank paper and clip these to the relevant grid as well.

The next stage is to 'mark up' your copy. This means to give instructions on how things will appear in print. Even if you are using a typewriter this is an essential stage. If you are using a computer you can dispense with this part of production, though in your initial stages of work you will certainly find this helpful.

Marking up is the provision of detailed instructions so that the individual producing the final, polished material will know exactly what you want. Essentially you need to instruct the person preparing the final type on the **typeface** you want, what size it should be and how wide the column should be.

Marking up for typewriters

If your newsletter uses typewriter text you will simply need to say what pitch typeface you want and how wide the column should be. The typist will then be able to set up their machine so that they produce exactly what you want. Providing you have done your copy fitting properly, what the typist provides you with should fit the space exactly.

Marking up for typesetters

If your newsletter is being produced by a typesetting company your mark-up needs to be more detailed. You will also have to learn a new 'language'. Apart from telling the typesetter which name of typeface you want, you will need to specify the size.

Type sizes

Type is measured in '**points**'. This is an ancient system of measurement dating back to the earliest printing presses in Europe. All you need to remember is that there are 72 points in one inch. So if you want type that is one inch high you will need to say '72pt'. However, as you may have guessed, it's not quite as simple as that. The measurement applies from the top of the highest ascender to the bottom of the lowest descender in the alphabet. Ascenders are the strokes of a character that poke upwards, such as the long side of the letter 'd'. Descenders are the long strokes that go below the line of type, as in a 'g'. Since the measurement is the distance between these extremes of the characters the normal letters will be smaller. So 72pt type will not in fact be one inch high. The distance between the top of the 'd' and the bottom of the 'p' will be one inch, so the letter 'a' may be only half an inch high. Figure 12 shows how type is measured.

Generally a newsletter will have type that is quite small. Characters which are only 8pt are quite readable. Indeed your daily newspaper probably uses type of 7pt. The size you use will depend

Fig. 12.   How to measure point size.

on the width of your column. The wider the column, the larger
the type size you require. If possible a column should contain
between 50 and 60 characters of your chosen typeface. For an A4
page with three columns this usually means type of around 10pt.
For a two column page you will need 11pt or 12pt. For a four
column page you will need 8pt or 9pt.

Leading
This is pronounced 'ledding' and is another ancient printing term.
It refers to the amount of space you want to insert between lines
of type. In the past this was achieved by the insertion of strips of
the metal lead between the rows of metal type. Hence the practice
became known as 'leading' the copy. Nowadays the term is still
used, even though hot metal printing is almost non-existent.

When you give your instructions to your typesetter you will need
to specify the amount of leading you require. If you do not specify
any leading the typesetter will 'set it solid'. In other words there
will be no space between the rows of type. Consequently, the
descenders of one row could touch the ascenders of the row below.
This makes the type harder to read, looks untidy and also reduces
the amount of white space on a page. This puts readers off and
you reduce the chances of communicating your message as a result.

So make sure that you give a precise amount of leading. In
general you should allow at least one point of extra space between
lines. However, the requirement varies according to the type design
you are using. Ask your typesetter for some samples so you can
choose the best looking type for the newsletter you are producing.

To mark up type for your typesetter you simply write the size
of the type you want, followed by a stroke, followed by the size of

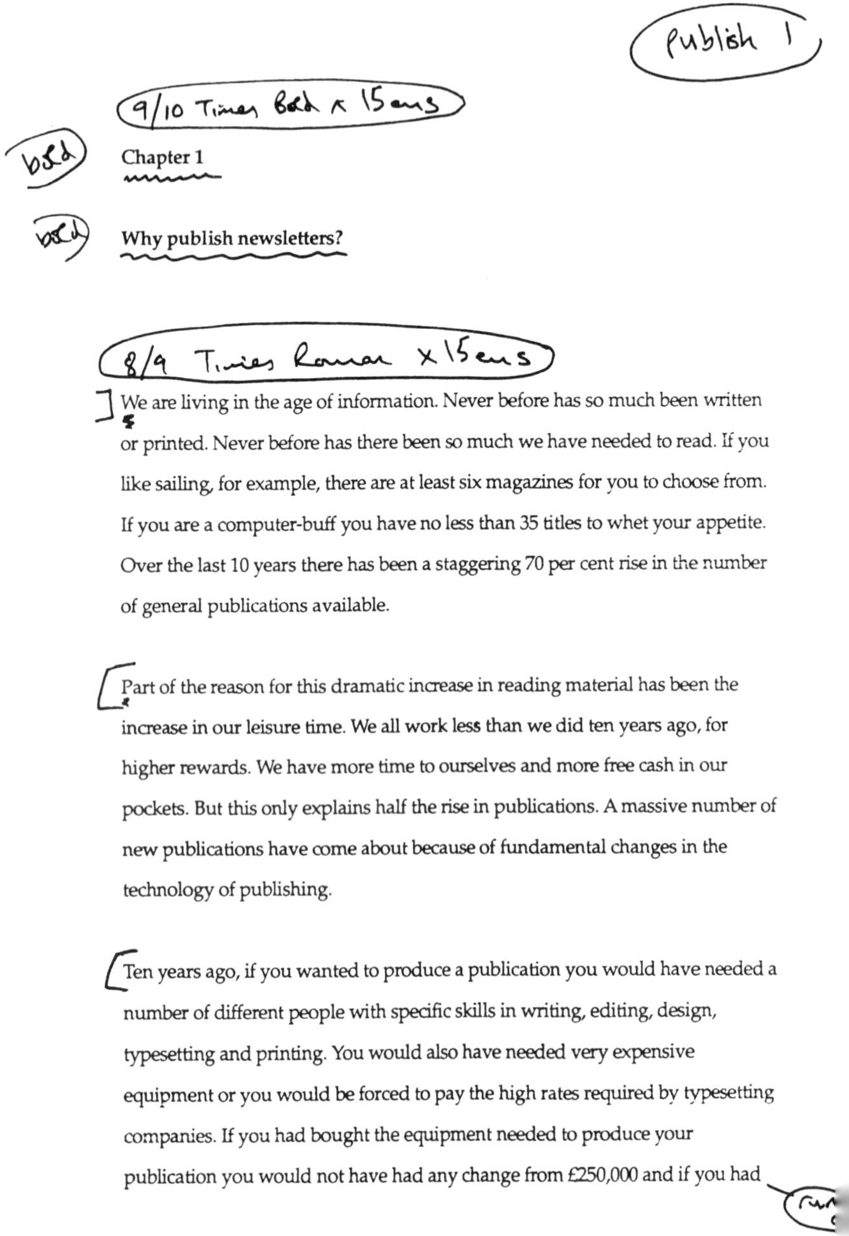

publish 1

9/10 Times Bold × 15 ems

bld

Chapter 1

ital

Why publish newsletters?

8/9 Times Roman × 15 ems

We are living in the age of information. Never before has so much been written or printed. Never before has there been so much we have needed to read. If you like sailing, for example, there are at least six magazines for you to choose from. If you are a computer-buff you have no less than 35 titles to whet your appetite. Over the last 10 years there has been a staggering 70 per cent rise in the number of general publications available.

Part of the reason for this dramatic increase in reading material has been the increase in our leisure time. We all work less than we did ten years ago, for higher rewards. We have more time to ourselves and more free cash in our pockets. But this only explains half the rise in publications. A massive number of new publications have come about because of fundamental changes in the technology of publishing.

Ten years ago, if you wanted to produce a publication you would have needed a number of different people with specific skills in writing, editing, design, typesetting and printing. You would also have needed very expensive equipment or you would be forced to pay the high rates required by typesetting companies. If you had bought the equipment needed to produce your publication you would not have had any change from £250,000 and if you had

run

Fig. 13.   Typesetting instructions.

leading you require, followed by the name of the typeface you want used. So your mark-up may look like this:

9/10pt Times Roman

Column widths

You now need to tell your typesetter what width you want the setting measured across. Here again you need to learn a new language. Typesetters measure the width of columns in a system known as '*pica ems*'. This also stretches back to printing in the middle-ages involving hot metal. All you need to worry about is that one pica em is equal to one sixth of an inch. If you have a three-column page your columns will measure around 12 or 13 pica ems. A four-column page will have columns measuring 10 pica ems and a two-column page will have columns around 15 pica ems. They will vary according to the actual size of your margins and the space you want between columns.

When you mark up your copy it should now read as follows:

9/10 Times Roman x 12

This tells the typesetter to set the type 9pts high on a leading of 10pts (ie an extra one point between the lines) in the typeface called Times Roman across a column width of 12 pica ems.

You will notice in Figure 13 that the instructions to the typesetter are drawn around with an oval shape. This is another instruction and means 'don't print me'. Anything circled off in this way will not be typeset.

Pica rules

If you want to be accurate about the widths of your columns you can buy a '**pica rule**'. This is a ruler where the units are pica ems so you can accurately measure your pages. Such rulers are not widely available. However, large artists' supplies shops will stock them or be able to order them for you. Also any Letraset dealer should be able to order these specialist rulers.

Marking up for computers

If you are using computers for the production of your newsletter much of this marking up will become irrelevant. The computer uses the same information as you would give to a typesetter, but instead gives a single name or 'stylesheet' to the mark-up instruction. So:

9/10pt Times Roman x 12 becomes

Body copy.

If you have copy presented to you in a variety of forms it is a good idea to physically mark up the text with the names of the style sheets you want applied. If all the copy is in the computer in the form of word processor files you can insert the name of the style sheet you want applied at the beginning of the text. This is called 'tagging' and the way you do it varies from program to program. However, it is well worth doing as it saves a great deal of production time. When you import the word processor text into the desktop publishing program it is automatically put into the style in which you want it to appear.

Where should I put instructions?
Your instructions, whether to a typist, a typesetter or a computer operator will need to be at the top of each page of type. The instructions will also need to be on each of the headline sheets you wrote out after completing your grid work. In this way you reduce the chances of errors occurring. To make sure that your material is definitely in the typeface and size you require you can repeat the instructions on the grid as in Figure 14.

Getting help with type
If you need some help to see various typefaces and various sizes ask your typesetter for a **type spec sheet**. This is a document which shows the various typefaces available in a variety of sizes. You will then be able to select the ones you like most and which will appeal to your readership, as defined in your psychological profile. If you are using a computer you can buy *The PostScript Font Manual*, which provides details of most of the popular typefaces available for computers.

PASTING UP

Paste-up is the essence of production of any publication. It is the

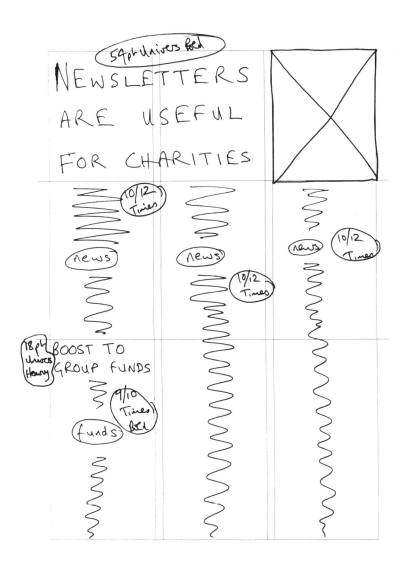

Fig. 14.   Stating typefaces and size requirements on the grid.

physical task of transferring your edited, typeset copy to the right position on the page according to your design.

When your typing is done, or when the typesetting is produced it will be in long strips. These are known as **galleys**. You must now measure the galleys very carefully and cut them up into the required sizes for each page. You will need to do this because some articles will be running across more than one column and you will need to cut up the long strip of typeset text into the required lengths for each column. Although you can use scissors for this job you will find it easier to use a scalpel. You can get these from artists' supply shops or from schools' suppliers who provide them for dissection kits. As a last resort ask your doctor for one!

Now that your material is in the right size you must stick it onto a blank sheet of paper accurately. If you want to be very accurate your printer will be able to supply you with **blues**. These are replicas of your grids on thick paper with the grid lines in a faint blue. This colour does not reproduce in the printing process, so you can use these lines to accurately position the pieces of text. Once the items are stuck down, smooth them carefully. You may find that a soft roller from a hardware store helps with this task. Bubbles will affect the reproduction, so they must be removed. However, be careful; typesetting is fragile material and rubbing over it with a hard ruler will affect it. To avoid too much damage you should use a glue known as 'Spray Mount', which is available in most stationery and artists' suppliers. Be careful when using it, make sure you are in a well ventilated area. The beauty of this glue is that it is not a permanent adhesive. So if the strip of typesetting is inaccurately placed or has bubbles in it, you can lift it off the backing sheet and reposition it.

If you have used photographs these too will need sticking down. If you are going to litho printing, though, you should not use the original pictures. Your typesetting company should have processed the pictures into **halftones**. These are printed on the same sort of paper as the text and can then be stuck down in the right position on the page. If your printing company is going to process the pictures simply leave a blank space in the appropriate part of the page.

Your first paste-up
If you have never done a paste-up before, do not use the original typesetting or typing. Instead, use a photocopy so that you can

make sure you have got things right. If you damage the originals all the work will have to be done again and you will be charged double. In fact, many typesetting companies only provide you with photocopied galleys. You do the paste up with these and the expert composition staff at the typesetting company simply copy your plan. If the typesetting company damages the galleys they bear the responsibility of correcting the mistake.

Electronic paste-up

Desktop publishing programs are nothing more than electronic paste-up systems. The text in a word processor is like a galley; the pictures in the image programs are like halftones. All you do with the computer is to place the items on the page according to your hand-drawn design. This is by far the most effective and productive way to use computerised publishing systems.

Handling artwork

The final page of pasted up text and pictures is now called '**artwork**'. This is the page from which your printer will work. Even if your newsletter is being photocopied this basic page is your artwork.

Artwork is precious. Do not cover it in fingerprints or coffee stains. Protect your artwork by taking the following steps:

● Mount the artwork on a thick piece of card (artists' supply shops provide exactly what you need).

● Cover the artwork with a sheet of paper attached to the card (an overlay).

● Store the artwork in a vertical filing system. Do not pile pieces of artwork on top of each other.

Sending artwork to printers

Once your artwork is produced and protected you will need to send it to the copying shop or to your printing company. Make sure that each page of artwork is clearly identified with the following items:

● title of newsletter
● page number

- publication date of newsletter
- publisher of newsletter
- address of publisher
- phone number of publisher
- delivery deadline.

Attach to each page a photocopy of the artwork, with special instructions for colours or position of colour photographs marked. Also attach the pictures to be included with each page.

Make sure you bundle all the pages together and tie them up with elastic or string. In this way the printer is less likely to lose a page of artwork.

If you produce artwork from your computer, whether it is laser printed or set from an imagesetting machine, you should still follow these rules. Many newsletters have their sparkle reduced because the artwork has been prepared poorly.

COMPUTERS AND PRODUCTION

Nowadays, more and more people will be using computers to produce their newsletters. Indeed, as was mentioned in Chapter 1, this is part of the reason for the increased publication of newsletters. Throughout this book there have been occasional references to computerised working. You should have realised by now that many of the steps taken to produce newsletters are common to every kind of production system. You should not think that because you use a computer system you will be able to avoid things like copy editing or drawing up a rough design on a grid. Such items are essential to the successful newsletter, no matter what production system is used.

What sort of computer should I have?

I am frequently asked which computer system is best for newsletters. There can be no single answer to that question. There are too many variables and each individual circumstance will require a different desktop publishing set-up. All I can say is get proper advice from independent publishing consultants and shop around. At the end of the day, however, after careful analysis of all the systems available over the years, I find that Aldus PageMaker is the most appropriate program for newsletter production on a computer. Another program called QuarkXPress would be my second choice for newsletters. If you cannot afford these programs, then I suggest TimeWorks, PageMaker Classic, Microsoft Publisher or Page Plus.

Whatever desktop publishing system you select, remember to get trained. You cannot simply open the box and get going. You will make mistakes and take four times as long as necessary to do anything. Training is widely available and every desktop publishing dealer provides it.

Computers are just a tool

Once you are trained you will find that you use the programs as a production tool. You will still need to follow all the instructions for producing the newsletter that have been given throughout this book. Desktop publishing systems are little more than a tool for doing the paste-up without getting your fingers sticky. If you can think of these machines in that sense, your newsletters will be much more successful. The trouble with the increase in desktop published newsletters over recent years is that the editors have thought they can do the entire job on the computer. This has meant they have missed out some vital aspects of the job of producing a successful newsletter. Your newsletter will be successful if your computer is used for only around 20% of the work.

Although computers will certainly help, and will dramatically reduce the time taken to produce your newsletter, do not think of them as the be-all and end-all. They are just a tool.

POINTS TO CONSIDER

1. How could you improve your own computer skills?

2. How can you spot the difference between a serif and sans serif typeface?

3. What are the main points to remember when handling artwork?

4. What point size do you think the text of this book is set in?

8
Distributing Your Newsletter

No matter how much effort you put into producing your newsletter your work will be in vain unless you can get your publication to your readers. Distribution is fundamental to your success. It is vital that you thoroughly investigate the available distribution options and ensure that copies of your newsletter are delivered to the right people at the right time. If your distribution system is weak, your newsletter will fail, no matter how good your copy editing has been.

TYPES OF DISTRIBUTION

For newsletters there are three main types of distribution:

- personal delivery
- mailings
- bulk dropping.

Personal delivery

In this system of distribution you or your colleagues physically hand out copies to your readers. Personal delivery can be used by in-house newsletters since you can give out copies at staff meetings, or put a copy on everyone's desk. You can also use personal delivery for your club newsletter by handing out copies at meetings. Personal delivery is also possible for local newsletters by popping copies through letterboxes.

Advantages
The main advantage of personal delivery is that you are certain your readers have received copies. Personal delivery is also generally the cheapest form of distribution.

Disadvantages

This system is only suitable for small print runs as handing out large numbers of newsletters is time consuming. Personal delivery also means it is easy to miss out giving copies to people on holiday or away for any other reason.

Mailings

This is by far the most popular system of distributing newsletters. You can use this for almost any kind of newsletter, even sending staff newsletters to your colleagues at their home address.

Advantages

The good thing about mailing is that you can deliver a copy of your newsletter direct to your readers without having to spend a great deal of time handing out copies. Mailings also mean you can distribute large numbers of newsletters easily. Another benefit of mailings is that you can enclose other material within the envelope, such as loose insert advertisements.

Disadvantages

Clearly one of the problems with mailings is the cost. This was covered in detail in Chapter 3. Another difficulty with a mailing system is that you must be sure your addresses are accurate. This means you must constantly maintain your mailing list and ensure that all changes are recorded immediately. A further difficulty with mailings is the need to do the physical task of stuffing newsletters in envelopes. If you decide not to do this yourself, you then need to find a suitable agency which can take on the work and you will need to keep an eye on them to be sure that they are maintaining a high level of service.

Bulk dropping

This is the form of distribution where you put large piles of copies in strategic sites so that your readers passing by can pick up a copy. This is useful for people in clubs and societies or for staff newsletters. It can also be used by companies who have lots of visitors, such as shops.

Advantages

This is a cheap way of distribution, though there will be some cost considerations (covered in Chapter 3) if you have more than one site at which newsletters can be picked up. The other advantage of bulk drops is that they involve you in the least amount of work. All you have to do is take your pile of copies to the strategic position and leave them there.

Disadvantages
You are entirely dependent on your readers actually picking up a copy. This means that you will miss getting copies to a portion of your potential readership who simply ignore the pile. Another disadvantage is that you need to remove out-dated copies from your distribution sites when you bring out a new issue. This means you have the problem of throwing away unwanted copies.

WHICH METHOD SHOULD I USE?

Determining which method of distribution is best for your newsletter will depend upon a variety of factors. These include:

- geographical spread of readers
- frequency of publication
- expectations of readers
- budget.

Geographical spread of readers
If your readers are all located in one area you could consider personal delivery. If your readers are widespread, but in discrete areas such as branches of your company, you could consider bulk dropping. If your readers are all over the place, mailings are likely to be the best method.

Frequency of publication
You are not likely to want to use a personal delivery system if your publication comes out daily. A mailed newsletter may be more appropriate, or bulk dropping as national newspapers do. However, if your newsletter comes out monthly or less frequently, personal delivery may not be such a problem. But if your newsletter is infrequent, perhaps once a quarter, you will not do well with bulk dropping. In the gap between editions your readers are likely to forget about the newsletter and will therefore not look out for the pile of copies three months later.

Expectations of readers

Your psychological profile will have given you some clues as to what your readers are like and how they might react to various methods of distribution. Indeed in your basic market research you may like to ask potential readers what type of distribution they would prefer. If your readers want to be mailed a copy they will not look for issues on bulk dropped piles. Similarly, if they expect to see piles of copies in the canteen at work, they will not take too kindly to being mailed a copy at home. You will need to take into account the wishes of your particular readers before settling on the best method of distribution.

Budget

The costs of the various distribution methods were discussed in detail in Chapter 3. You should be sure that you have carefully calculated the budgetary implications of your chosen method of distribution and compared the alternatives.

COMBINED DISTRIBUTION

I am very much in favour of newsletters using combined methods of distribution. In other words you can use all three main methods of getting newsletters to your readers. By combining personal delivery, mailings and bulk droppings you provide a belt and braces approach to getting your newsletter to your readers.

Case history: The estate agent

Tony Smythe has now completed his first newsletter, thanks to the assistance of his friend from the local paper in Goldmead. Now it is time to distribute the first edition. Tony has carefully considered the methods of distribution, and has decided to combine three different ways of getting newsletters out to his readers.

The main supply of newsletters will be personally delivered to everyone living in the Westfield area. The newsletter will be popped through the letterbox of every house by his two assistants over two evenings. Tony has agreed to pay each assistant £20 overtime for this work.

Tony has also decided to do some 'bulk drops' of the newsletter. He intends placing some 100 copies on the bar of the Bat and Ball pub. He will also have 100 copies on the front desk of his estate agency office. A further 100 copies will be in the entrance to the village hall and 50 copies will be in the waiting room at the doctor's surgery.

The third method of distribution will be mailing. Tony has decided to mail a copy to everyone who is looking for a house in the Westfield area. He has 75 interested customers at the moment, so the mailing can be handled in-house. He calculates the cost to be £32.25 for the stamps and envelopes. The mailing can easily be handled by his secretary, Alison, during office hours.

With the money for overtime to his assistants and the cost of the mailing, the total distribution bill is going to be £72.25. Tony has rounded this budget up to £100 to allow for entertainment of the landlord of the pub, the doctor and the caretaker of the village hall who have all cooperated in the distribution.

The lessons learned

By combining a number of methods of distribution, Tony has made sure that all of his potential readers see a copy. Although everyone in the village will have a copy in their house, this doesn't mean that every member of the household will have read the newsletter. So by having additional copies in the three main community centres Tony has provided enough extras for everyone to have a chance to read the newsletter. Also, by mailing the newsletter to his potential customers Tony will have stimulated interest in the area and will therefore have made it more likely that people will want to buy a house in the region. By having copies on the front desk of his 'shop', Tony will be able to get copies to people who pop in, such as new potential customers who aren't yet on his mailing list. The result of Tony's distribution method is that everyone has been catered for. Had Tony followed his original plan of just popping copies through the doors of local residents he would have missed many potential readers.

Case history: The Student Union

Steve Wilson at the Millchester Student Union has opted for a combined distribution method. His main method of delivery will be bulk drops. Piles of the newsletter will be placed in strategic places around the university campus. The newsletter will be put in the Student Union building, each of the bars of the student residences, the campus health centre, the university information office and the library.

Steve has also decided to add a second means of distribution, mailing. The newsletter will be mailed to past students who have taken up a subscription. It will also be mailed to key university personnel such as the Chancellor, the heads of academic departments, the senior administrators and the student tutors.

The cost of the mailing is estimated at £100.

The lessons learned
Although the Student Union is only using two methods of distribution, the combination has helped ensure that some key people are certain to get copies. Although the Chancellor and the student tutors could pick up copies in the library or some other place, mailing ensures they get their personal copy. In this way the Student Union is certain to convey important information to key members of the university staff. If Steve had relied solely on bulk dropping he may not have been able to be sure his newsletter was reaching the right people.

Advantages of combined distribution
No matter what type of newsletter you produce you can benefit from combined methods of distribution. Let's take some examples of how the system could work. Combined distribution could help:

- staff newsletters
- company newsletters
- club/society newsletters.

Distributing staff newsletters
For staff newsletters you could consider a combination of bulk drops and mailings. Put your staff newsletter in strategic sites around your company, such as staff rooms, canteens, social clubs and the like. But also make sure you mail the newsletter to the key managers and senior members of staff. In this way you will be communicating to the people who can influence the way the company is run. If your company is relatively small you may also want to use personal delivery by placing copies on everyone's desk or work station.

Distributing company newsletters
If you produce a company newsletter which is aimed at your customers and potential customers, you should consider a com-

bination of all three of the main methods of distribution. Certainly all of your contacts should be mailed a copy.

You should also have bulk supplies in your shops and reception areas for anyone to pick up.

Personal delivery should also be considered. Have copies in your briefcase at all times and supply each of your company representatives with enough copies for all of their contacts. They can then hand out a copy of the newsletter personally. Many companies favour this method of distribution as the arrival of the new, interesting, newsletter is a good reason to suggest a new appointment with a potential customer. So if reps have newsletters with them at all times they can use them as 'door openers', a means of getting to see possible clients.

Distributing club/society newsletters
Many clubs and societies are able to use personal delivery for their newsletters. You can hand out copies at meetings and social gatherings.

But it is also worthwhile using bulk drops as well as, perhaps, mailings. You can place piles of the club newsletter in the entrance to your meeting hall or at sites where your club regulars meet.

You could also mail a copy to everyone in the society at their home address to be doubly sure they get a copy. Clubs and societies could also mail issues to key people who can influence their future. These might include local politicians, caretakers of meeting halls, potential new members and so on.

CHOOSING A DISTRIBUTION AGENT

No matter what type of distribution you choose you will probably need someone to help. The factors for consideration in choosing who depend upon the types of distribution you wish to use. Naturally, however, cost will be an influencing factor in all methods of distribution.

Personal delivery
If you are using personal delivery you will need willing helpers. These individuals must be physically capable of doing the work you require. They must also be polite and have a ready smile.

Nothing will do your newsletter more harm than a sullen, rude individual who looks bored and simply says 'here you are' when giving out your latest production. Readers will approach your newsletter in a much more positive frame of mind if your distributors smile, look happy and confident and hand over the newsletter with 'here's the latest copy of *The News*. The article on page 7 should interest you'.

One other point about personal distribution. You will need to make sure that the people who have agreed to help you are available to fit in with your schedule. Do not use people who can't make it on Wednesday evenings, for instance, if you want your newsletter out mid-week. It sounds obvious, but these are the little things so easily forgotten which can be the downfall of a newsletter.

Organising mailings

If you are going to use mailings you should get the *Post Office Direct Mail Handbook*. This is not available from the Post Office! It is a normal book, sold in book shops, though you will probably have to order it. You should also get the *Royal Mail Business Mailguide* from Royal Mail House, 148-166 Old Street, London EC1V 9HQ. This provides details of the various mailing services from the Post Office, together with a guide on the prices you will be charged. If you do the mailings yourself this book will be a vital guide to ensure you get the delivery service you want at the right price.

However, you may not wish to do the mailing yourself. You may need the assistance of external mailing agencies if your newsletter is a large print run or you just do not have the time or facilities. (Even sticking on 200 stamps can be time consuming and tongue-wearing.) Mailing agencies can be found in *Yellow Pages*. It is always a good idea to choose a company near to you or your printer. Indeed, your printing firm will be able to advise you on mailing services in their area. Many print companies are asked to handle distribution so they know about mailing houses in their neck of the woods.

Choosing a mailing agency is a bit like choosing a printing company. You need to let three or more agencies know exactly what you want and then compare their prices and terms of business. To let the companies know what you want you should use the form in Figure 15.

MAILING QUOTATION REQUEST	
Quotation required for mailing a newsletter	
Number of copies	
Maximum physical size of copies	
Weight of one copy (in grammes)	
Type of envelopes required	
Labels will/will not be supplied	
Postage class required	
Mailings to take place weekly/monthly/quarterly	
Delivery of copies to you on: (dates)	
Mailings required by: (dates)	

Fig. 15.   Information you should supply to a mailing agency.

Once you get your quotations back you can decide which company to use.

Mailing houses will offer a variety of other services, including handling your mailing list and wrapping the newsletter in clear plastic film instead of an envelope. You should always consider the options on offer from mailing houses and judge whether they are appropriate for your newsletter. Always ask your mailing house to show you samples of their work, such as labels and envelopes. You do not want your newsletter arriving in a tatty looking cover. So get the mailing right.

Bulk dropping
If you want to bulk drop your newsletter you may only need some trusty helpers who are capable of carrying a heavy box of newsletters to the appropriate distribution points. However, if your

newsletter is going to a number of widespread distribution points you may need the assistance of a specialist delivery company. Usually the easiest way to cope with such bulk drops is to pass the work on to your printer. You simply tell the printing company how many copies are required for each address. Most printing companies have their own delivery vans and will do the work for you. Others will need the assistance of a nationwide delivery company like Interlink or Omega. If they use such agents you will be charged the delivery fee plus a small mark-up. This may be acceptable; however, you could always ask a delivery company for a quote yourself to compare the price from your printer. But if you are getting bulk dropping done from your office you will need space to store the supply of newsletters which arrive from the printers. You will also add a day or two to the distribution process which could have been avoided had the job been done by your printing company.

CHECKING DISTRIBUTION

Without efficient distribution your newsletter will fail, so you need a system of checking. The way to do this is to put your home address on any mailing list. You will then be able to monitor the way the mailing was done and the dates on which delivery was effected. This is the usual way of keeping your eye on mailing houses.

If you rely on bulk drops, make sure you visit the centres at random to ensure that the deliveries are being made properly.

If you use personal delivery there is no adequate way of ensuring your agents are popping the newsletters through letterboxes instead of dumping them all over a hedge. One way of finding out if this is happening is to include a competition in your newsletter. You should be able to monitor the levels of entry and if a contest has a sudden drop you will suspect that some copies didn't get delivered!

Distribution rules OK

Whatever kind of newsletter you produce, remember the rule that distribution is king. Without distribution which is effective and efficient you will lose readers and your newsletter will surely die. Even if you have to bend some of the other suggestions in this book to suit your particular needs, do not skimp on ensuring effective distribution.

9
The Law and Newsletters

Anyone can become a publisher and sell or distribute their own newsletter. There is no legal requirement to establish a company nor is there any need to register with a professional body or institute. You just start up and go. However, you will soon find yourself in difficulties if you fall foul of any of the following laws:

- copyright
- libel
- obscenity
- imprinting.

COPYRIGHT

Everything that is written down is protected by copyright. There is no requirement to 'publish' the material. So the shopping list I wrote last Saturday is protected and I can sue if anyone picks it up out of the bin and duplicates it! Everything that is written down is automatically protected by the **Copyright, Designs and Patents Act 1988**. This new act replaced all previous laws, so if you have any old books on copyright they will not be much use to you nowadays.

The essence of copyright

Copyright is there to protect originality. Without a copyright law we could freely copy each other's work. This would reduce the desire to write anything original if you knew that it could immediately be ripped off without so much as a 'thank you' to the first writer. Copyright protects the rights of an individual in the written word. Something which is written down is property, according to the Act, and so it may be sold or rented according to the wishes of the owner. If someone uses the words without the explicit permission of the owner this is seen as tantamount to theft and so recompense is available.

Copyright and your sources

Everything that you receive for your newsletter is protected by copyright, of course. This means other publications you subscribe to, radio programmes you listen to, notes from your contributors and the articles you commission. Anything that is written down and given to you is protected by copyright. You do not have the rights to use the material in your newsletter unless you have obtained permission from the copyright owner.

Rights available

Just as you can decide whether to hire out your camera or not, so copyright owners can decide whether or not to let you use their material. There is a wide range of 'licences' available. Basically these boil down to:

- no reproduction rights
- single reproduction rights
- all rights
- assignment.

No reproduction rights

This is self explanatory. The owner of the copyright has essentially forbidden you to use the material. You cannot reproduce the words at all. This will be the case for all the other publications to which you subscribe. In the small print you will see something like:

> 'No part of this publication may be reproduced in any means what-soever, stored in a retrieval system or copied in whole or in part.'

This means: 'hands off, it's mine'. If you do use the material you face prosecution, in just the same way as someone who takes your camera from you, in spite of you saying 'no', could be done for theft.

Single reproduction rights

This kind of licence is the most common from contributors. It means you can use the material they have provided for you once only in a single publication in one country. If you want to use the material in more than one newsletter or publish it in a number of countries you will need additional permission from the originator. Usually this means additional fees will need to be paid. If you reproduce the material outside the strict terms of the licence you are liable for prosecution for infringement of the law.

All rights
When you are given a licence for all rights you are allowed to reproduce the material as many times as you like, wherever you like, whenever your like. You don't need to pay any more money to the originator and you don't need extra permissions. You are unlikely to get an 'all rights' licence from most contributors unless you pay a large fee at the outset.

Assignment
This is different to all rights. With an all rights you can do what you like with the material but you don't actually own it. Essentially it is on permanent loan to you. With 'assignment' you have actually bought the material and it is now your property for you to deal with as you wish. Assignments can only be made in writing with a clear contract explicitly detailing the act of assignment. Such contracts are rare in the extreme and you are unlikely to ever have something assigned to you.

ACQUIRING RIGHTS

Many publishers are greedy. They want their contributors to give them all rights or even assign the copyright over to them. Such practice is largely frowned upon nowadays because it reduces creativity and originality. You should be a realist and simply attempt to acquire the rights you need and no more. In most instances this will be 'single rights'. To get such rights you need to be specific when requesting material for your newsletter. Even today many professional writers are naive about copyright and do not understand the law as it stands. If you do not make things clear at the outset there could be problems in the future, which can only be resolved by getting expensive legal opinions.

The way to get the rights you require is to issue every contributor with a 'commissioning letter'. This states clearly what you need and the rights you want to buy. It forms the contract between you and your contributor. A suitable commissioning letter is shown in Figure 16.

Dear Mike,

Further to my telephone conversation I would be grateful if you could write the article I requested for the next issue of *The Newsletter*. The details are set out below.

Article: A review of the annual meeting
Length: 750 words
Deadline: 15th October 199X
Copyright: Single reproduction rights in one issue of *The Newsletter*. We to have first publishing rights. You retain all other rights.
Fee £100 payable within 30 days of invoice.
Other details: Please supply the copy on disk in Word Perfect as
  agreed.

I hope all this is acceptable.

Best wishes

Fig. 16.   Typical commissioning letter.

As you can see the letter is short and to the point and makes it clear the rights you want to buy. The letter mentions first rights, indicating that the editor wants to be able to publish the material before any other publication. This means the contributor can sell the material again if he or she wants to but only after publication in *The Newsletter*.

When you don't need commissioning letters

You will not need a commissioning letter, unless you want one for the record, when you are producing a newsletter in-house and the contributor is an employee of the company. The 1988 Act established the fact that material written in the course of employment is the copyright of the employer. In other words there is automatic assignment of copyright from employees to employers in any written material produced as part of their work. So if you produce a staff newsletter and you commission an article from another member of staff you are free to do what you like with the material, even sell it outside, without the need for permission from the author. However, whether it is politic to do that only you can judge depending on your particular situation.

What you mustn't do with your source material
Providing you have made it clear in any commissioning letters what you want to do with contributions, you can do exactly what the agreed terms of the licence are. However, you must not go beyond the bounds of the licence you have acquired. In most cases this means you must not:

● sell the article elsewhere
● use the article more than once
● publish the article outside the UK.

Also, because you will almost certainly not have any kind of rights in material included in other publications, you must not:

● copy material, words or pictures, from other publications.

Penalties for infringement
If you break any of the rules about copyright you could find yourself in court. Copyright is both a civil and criminal offence so you might end up in two courts! If you break the law of copyright the owner of the material can sue you for damages. The penalties awarded are unlimited, so the more damage the offended individual can claim, the more cash you will need to find. Because it is also a criminal offence to infringe copyright you can find yourself being fined or at worst, imprisoned for up to two years.

COPYRIGHT AND YOUR NEWSLETTER

Because there is copyright in everything which is printed, your newsletter also acquires rights. Although you will not necessarily have bought all rights in the articles you publish, you will certainly have all rights in the way they are presented. So your copyright ownership forbids anyone to photocopy the pages of your news-letter, for example. This applies even to the authors of the articles. They own the copyright in the words themselves, but you own the copyright in the way the page has been put together.

As an example, I own the copyright in the words printed in this book. I have given How To Books Ltd the exclusive licence to print these words anywhere in the world and also to be able to sell a variety of associated rights in the words, such as serialisations. But at the end of the day I still own the words and How To Books Ltd has to pay me fees for any associated rights it sells on my behalf. However, if I were to photocopy a page of this book I would be infringing the copyright of How To Books Ltd in the page itself and the company could sue me.

So you own the entire copyright in your newsletter and can do with it what you like, providing you do not infringe any of the terms of the copyright licences you have acquired. There is one exception to this. The copyright in the newsletter will be retained by your employers if you produce the publication as part of your job.

In any event, you can sue if people copy your newsletter or extract parts of it. Keep your eye open for regular thieves and ensure they get a stiff letter from your lawyer.

LIBEL

If you think copyright is complex, wait until you hear about libel! Libel is the law protecting people from defamation of their character when the offending matter is published. This is different to slander, which applies merely to the spoken word. Your newsletter should be careful not to libel anyone or you could find yourself involved in lengthy and costly legal cases.

Who can you libel?

You can only libel living individuals, you cannot libel the dead. Neither can you libel companies or products or other objects. There are some very minor exceptions to this, such as when your criticism of a company damages its trading position, but libel is almost always about offending living individuals.

How do you libel someone?

To commit a libel they must first prove that you published something. The Defamation Act of 1956 suggests that publication is showing something to a third party. So if I write a potentially libellous memo to you about you, it is not an actionable offence unless that memo is allowed to be seen by a third individual. In other words you have got to send something to someone other than the person being criticised before it can become libellous.

If the act of publication can be proved the offended individual then needs to show that the material is **defamatory**. The classic definition is that the words must have exposed the person to 'hatred, contempt or ridicule', but new definitions are added all the time. So if you lower the person in the 'estimation of right thinking members of society' you could also have committed a defamation. Another definition is that the words 'would be likely to affect a person adversely in the estimation of reasonable people generally'. You can also libel someone by reducing their status within their profession.

Even if someone can prove all these things, though, and show that you actually published the words, they still need to be able to prove the words were about them. In other words, the offending article must clearly have referred to the complainant otherwise libel is not proven.

Defences againat libel
The main defences are:

● justification
● fair comment
● absolute privilege
● qualified privilege.

There are two others of 'leave and licence' and 'innocent defamation', but these are very rarely used.

Justification
You can defend yourself against a libel action if you can prove the article was true in substance and fact. This is a difficult defence as you will need to prove all of the facts in your material and will need to show that they were all completely truthful.

Fair comment
This is by far the most common defence. Providing the material complained about was actual comment you can claim that the words were published objectively, fairly and in the public interest without malicious intent.

Absolute privilege
This defence applies to only a limited number of cases. It is a

complete defence and is rarely used. However, you can claim absolute privilege if you edit the proceedings of Parliament, or report judicial proceedings.

Qualified privilege
You can claim qualified privilege when your article is a report of Parliamentary proceedings, reports on judicial proceedings some time after the case, or where there is a moral, legal or social duty to communicate the information.

Avoiding libel

As you can see, libel is complex. Indeed the lawyers who deal with libel are specialists and rarely handle other kinds of cases. As a result they charge very high fees. If you are accused of libel you will need to pay a large legal bill, even if you win the case out of court! Most cases do not end up in court and in spite of headline awards in recent years, few complainants are awarded more than £10,000 damages. Even so, this could cripple your newsletter, especially when you add on all the legal costs. You will therefore want to avoid libel.

To avoid libel check all your articles for truth. If they are true, and you can prove it, do not worry about libel too much. If the material contains opinion, which you cannot prove as true by its very nature, you will need to check to see whether the comment is fair and objective. If it is just sniping or sour grapes, cut it out of the article. The maxim of editors should always be:

if in doubt, cut it out.

If you are still doubtful about an article, get it checked by a lawyer. Your solicitor chum, or the company lawyer are unlikely to be able to help. Their knowledge of libel could well be less than yours. Instead, get a specialist to help. A good way of finding someone with some additional knowledge is to contact your local newspaper. They will retain a lawyer who advises them and would be happy to give you the details so you can get your article checked. It may cost you around £100 to get the words checked over, but that is a small price to pay compared with a six-figure bill when you end up in the High Court.

Libel insurance

It is possible to get yourself insured against libel. Premiums are high and you will need to consider setting aside several thousand pounds for good cover. A company which specialises in libel insurance is Sun Alliance and your local branch will put you in touch with the specialists.

OBSCENITY

This is a difficult area. What is obscene to one person is not obscene to another. There is no real consensus on obscenity. The current definition is something which could 'deprave and corrupt' an open mind. Quite what that means is open to interpretation. *Lady Chatterley's Lover* was obscene once yet now it is an 'A' level textbook. Pictures of naked couples apparently having sexual intercourse were once obscene, but now such scenes have been included in TV plays. The important point about obscenity is that it does not just cover pictures.

Words can be obscene as well. Generally most newsletters are unlikely to publish anything which is obscene. However, if in doubt about pictures or text you intend to carry, you should seek legal advice.

IMPRINTING

An 'imprint' is a legal requirement on your newsletters. Under the **Newspapers, Printers and Reading Rooms Repeal Act 1869** and the **Printer's Imprint Act 1961** you must include on either the front, the back or inside the front, the name and address of the printing company which produced the newsletter. The reason for this provision is so that anyone seeking redress against what has been published has someone to contact. Usually an imprint also contains the name and address of the publisher, though there is no legal requirement to do this. If you do not publish a proper imprint you face the risk of prosecution. The maximum penalty is a £50 fine for each copy of each edition which does not carry the imprint. If your newsletter had a print run of just 100 copies this would be a £5,000 fine! So beware; always put the name and address of the printer on your newsletter. Cases for non-imprinting are heard regularly, so you do risk being prosecuted.

OTHER LEGAL ISSUES

Although copyright, libel, obscenity and imprinting are major concerns for publishers of newsletters, there are other legal areas which you need to be aware of.

Legal deposit

Every publication must by law be deposited with the British Library. A blind eye is turned to small publications, brochures and the like. But if your newsletter is regular and substantial in terms of circulation and pagination you should send a copy to the British Library. You should send your copies to:

Legal Deposit Office
British Library
Boston Spa
Wetherby
West Yorkshire LS23 7BY

ISSN

Although this is not a legal requirement, you can get an International Standard Subscription Number for your newsletter. You get the numbers from:

UK National Serials Data Centre
British Library
Boston Spa
Wetherby
West Yorkshire LS23 7BY

Using this number identifies your newsletter to librarians and publication specialists. As a result you can widen your readership. If you get an ISSN for your newsletter you must place it on the front cover of each copy, preferably on the top right of the page.

Competitions

There are laws governing competitions, so if you hold any reader contests you must ensure they are legal. Essentially they must be real and the prizes offered must actually be given out. There must also be an element of skill in the competition, but you cannot ask entrants to predict future events or say what past results will be if that result is not yet known. If you want to run a bingo game the prizes must be distributed by pure chance and no purchase must be necessary for someone to enter. One other thing about competitions is that you should store all the entries for three years after the closing date. If someone disputes the result this is the amount of time they have available in which to raise an action. You would need the original entries to back your case. If you fall foul of any competition laws you could risk fines up to £2,000 or up to two years in prison.

Racial hatred

Under the **Public Order Act 1936** you could commit an offence if you publish anything which is threatening, abusive or insulting for particular races or ethnic groups. In other words you mustn't stir up trouble against any racial group in any article you publish. If you do not abide by this rule you can only be prosecuted after authorisation of the case by the Attorney General, which is rare.

Contempt of court

This is a complex law and a controversial one as well. Contempt of court is a criminal action and usually results in very heavy fines or imprisonment of offenders. You would commit contempt of court if anything you publish 'creates a substantial risk that the course of justice in particular proceedings will be substantially impeded or prejudiced'. If your newsletter ever covers material about legal cases, or even potential legal cases, you risk contempt of court. You should seek expert legal advice to ensure you do not commit an offence.

GETTING LEGAL HELP

The law relating to the media is quite complex and very specialist. You are unlikely to get good assistance from your own solicitor or company lawyer. You should always seek specialist help. As already mentioned, local newspapers retain lawyers who have a specialist knowledge of media issues. Seeking out these solicitors is a good idea. Also the large legal firms will have their own experts, usually based in London, but you can still get assistance from your nearby office.

You should also read *Law and the Media* by Tom G Crone, Heinemann Professional Publishing. This is an excellent guide to modern law and provides a basic grounding for anyone producing a newsletter.

THE LEGAL HEALTH CHECK

If you are producing your own newsletter and want to quickly check that you are unlikely to fall into legal hot water, take the following legal health check for all your articles.

1. Do I have the right to publish this material?
2. Are the facts in this article true?
3. Is the comment in this article fair?
4. Is the article balanced?
5. Would the material be acceptable to my friends?
6. Is this material unlikely to offend my colleagues?
7. Am I happy with this article?

If you can answer 'yes' confidently to all of these questions you are unlikely to have a great deal of legal difficulty. However, this health check is not intended to replace proper legal opinion. Neither is there any guarantee associated with this health check. It is merely provided to show you the sort of questions you must ask about every article or picture you intend to publish if you wish to reduce the chances of legal problems.

POINTS TO CONSIDER

1. What do you think would be the main legal risks faced by your own newsletter? What steps would you take to minimise them?

2. What imprint name will you use as publisher of the newsletter?

3. If you thought a proposed article might be defamatory, would you just cut out the offending piece, or discuss it with the contributor first?

10
The Next Issue

Few newsletters come out just once. Many are monthly, some are weekly and quite a few are daily. No sooner have you completed one issue than the printer seems to be calling for the artwork for the next one. Like any other aspect of newsletter production, unless you plan properly you will find the constant roller coaster of issue deadlines too daunting. You will become exhausted and your newsletter will be a flop. To ensure that this scenario does not arise you need proper planning.

THE EDITORIAL CONFERENCE

The essence of good publication planning is the editorial conference. If you are a daily newsletter this should be held every day. If you are weekly you may need a couple of these meetings a week. If you are a monthly one, every other week should suffice. If you are quarterly, once a month is generally all that is needed. However often you hold your editorial conference, this will be the kick start to the planning you need.

Who attends the conference?

Exactly who comes to the meeting depends upon the type of newsletter you are producing and who is involved. If you are in a publishing department of a large company there may be half a dozen people attending the meeting. If you are in a club or society there may only need to be you and the club chairman discussing things over lunch. Whatever format the meeting takes, make sure you have a regular slot in your diary for it.

What is the agenda?

The agenda for an editorial conference is always the same. The first item is the discussion of the previous issue. You need to look critically at the last issue. Ask yourself and your colleagues at the meeting the following questions:

- Did the articles make sense?
- Were the articles correctly targeted at your audience?
- Was the design acceptable?
- What could have been done to improve the issue?

Having critically analysed the issue you will be in a better position to proceed with the next one. If you do not criticise each issue you produce your standards will drop and you will lose readers, eventually killing off the publication.

The next item on the agenda is what material should be included in the next issue. Here your newsletter structure, developed in Chapter 4, will be of value. Ask all of the people at the meeting if they have ideas for each particular section of the newsletter. Make a note of every single idea. Do not at this stage reject anything.

The third item on your editorial conference agenda should be setting priorities. Go through the list of ideas and sort them into the order of importance. Quite how you arrive at this order will depend upon the type of newsletter you produce, but you should generally try to keep the most topical items at the top of the list.

Now you must decide how long each article should be. The length of an article is based on its value to the readers, the extent of the available information and the space you have in your newsletter. Compromises will have to be made in order to fit things into your structure, but this is no bad thing. Discipline will help you produce a better newsletter.

The final item to be discussed is the delegation of work. Having set your priorities of what you want covered, and how long the articles should be, you now allocate names of writers and deadline dates.

At the end of the editorial conference you should have a list which looks like that in Figure 17.

As you can see you should have a detailed outline of what will be in the next issue, who will contribute the required material, when the copy will be provided and how many words will be written. You may also have a similar list of requisitions for illustrations. You will notice also that there is a list of 'left overs'. These are ideas which have not yet been rejected and which may be suitable for future editions. These items can then be re-discussed

Editorial Conference
The Newsletter
12th September 199X

Previous issue
   Needed more pictures
   Some articles seemed too long (particularly the centre spread)
   The sports pages are too dominated by football

Action needed
   Each page must have one picture on it
   Maximum length of all articles is now 1,200 words
   Must search for contributors on tennis and hockey

Next issue
   Ideas:
      Tennis club 10th birthday
      Village hall redecoration finished
      Mayor's daughter getting married
      New plans for bypass approved
      Annual fete being planned
      Rotary club annual dinner
      New houses for west side of village
      Our shop extends opening hours

   Decisions

Bypass	Page 1	Susan	4th Oct	750 wds
Rotary club	Page 2	Susan	5th Oct	750 wds
Our new hours	Page 3	Me	5th Oct	500 wds
New houses	Page 4	Me	6th Oct	200 wds
Tennis club	Page 4	Gemma	5th Oct	450 wds

   Left overs
      Village hall redecoration
      Mayor's daughter's wedding
      Annual fete

Fig. 17. Editorial conference notes.

Forward Plan
Tony Smythe Estate Agents
FEBRUARY 199X
Focus on Goldmead sales
Profile of George Johnson
News of first time buyer properties

APRIL 199X
Focus on Goldmead wedding services
Profile of Anna Thomson
News of houses with swimming pools

JUNE 199X
Focus on Goldmead pubs
Profile of Martin Thursley
News of executive homes

AUGUST 199X
Focus on Westfield leisure
Profile of Cathy Ray
News of flats and studios

OCTOBER 199X
Focus on Goldmead restaurants
Profile of Ruth Armstrong
News of family homes

DECEMBER 199X
Focus on Goldmead Christmas lights/shopping
Profile of Gary Trail (this year's Santa!)
News of retirement properties

Fig. 18.   A typical forward plan.

at future editorial conferences and are there just in case you run
out of ideas in the future. If you don't store such ideas you could
be sitting in your conference thinking that you had a brilliant idea
for the political page a month ago, but what was it?

The editorial conference is the basis for future planning. It is the forum for ideas, none of which should be rejected without long consideration over a number of meetings.

FORWARD PLANS

With a few editorial conferences under your belt you will be able to produce a forward plan. This is a detailed list of all the items you intend publishing for the next year. Most magazines and newspapers produce such a plan as it is helpful in attracting advertising. If your newsletter is likely to accept adverts you will need to produce this forward plan as soon as you can. A typical forward plan is shown in Figure 18, for the estate agency case history.

IDEAS FOR FUTURE PLANS

Your editorial conference will provide plenty of ideas for your future plans. However, this may not be sufficient, especially if you are the only person at the editorial conference! You will need to think about other stimulants for ideas. These include:

- anniversaries
- seasons
- events
- birthdays.

You can link any article or theme to an anniversary of some kind or to the birthday of someone famous. You can also dream up article ideas for specific events that are already in your calendar. Or you can try linking articles to seasons. You do not just have to think about the standard four seasons. There are 'seasons' for house buying, car buying, holidays and romance. There are seasons for weddings and retirements as well as for dieting. In case you don't know them:

- most houses are bought in the period between April and June
- most cars are bought in August and September
- holidays occur in two peaks, August and March
- romantic purchases are made in April and May
- most weddings take place in September
- most retirements occur in August
- most diets are started in January.

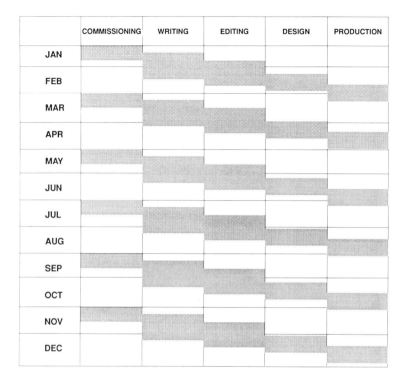

Fig. 19.   Chart for planning an annual schedule.

If you want to know more dates and anniversaries you need a good reference book such as *Chambers Dictionary of Dates.*

SCHEDULING

Just as it is important to schedule each issue, so you need to timetable your work for the year. No matter what the frequency of your newsletter, you will always be working on the next issue before the current one is finished. You will need to be thinking about commissioning articles for the next issue while arranging proof reading for the current issue and looking at the last issue for critical comments at the editorial conference. To help you plan your time you should draw up a chart like the one in Figure 19 which shows the annual schedule for the Student Union newsletter used in our case studies.

From this case study you can see that the schedule has a number of overlapping items. Your schedule is not likely to be the same but at least with a chart like this on your wall you know what you should be doing. Without an annual plan like this example you will feel overwhelmed by the conflicting amount of work and your newsletter will suffer.

A FINAL WORD

Newsletter publishing is exciting and interesting, but unless you plan ahead your efforts will be in vain. Your newsletter will not be published on time, you will lose readers, advertisers will lack confidence and you will get frustrated.

The key to a successful newsletter is thorough, in-depth planning. You may want to start producing your newsletter straight away. You will have more success if you sit back, think and gradually develop your ideas before rushing into things. I have been involved in newsletter publishing for many years and have seen plenty of failures along the way. All of those departed newsletters have been due to poor planning at some stage. The successful ones are those which had thorough, analytical and critical planning at the outset. Don't skimp on your plans, otherwise all the other advice I have given in this book will be to no avail.

Further Information

General

The Consultant's Guide to Newsletter Profits, Herman R. Holtz (Dow Jones-Irwin) USA 1987

Editing Your Newsletter, Mark Beach (Van Rostrand Reinhold) USA 1983

Guide to Self Publishing, Harry Mulholland (Mullholland-Wirral) 1984

How to Publish a Book, Robert Spicer (How To Books) 2nd edition 1995

How to Publish Yourself, Peter Finch (Allison and Busby) 1987

Magazine Journalism Today, Anthony Davis (Heinemman) 1988

Publishing and Printing at Home, Roy Lewis and John Easson (David and Charles) 1984

Publishing Your Own Specialist Magazine, Alan Greene (Kogan Page) 1990

Read All About It, James Derounian (Community Council of Devon) 1985

Finance

Book Keeping, Donald Cousins (Teach Yourself Books) 1983

Do Your Own Bookkeeping, Max Pullen (Kogan Page) 1988

Finance for Small Businesses, Keith Checkley (Sphere Reference) 1985

How to Keep Business Accounts, Peter Taylor (How To Books) 3rd edition 1995

How to Manage Budgets & Cash Flows, Peter Taylor (How To Books) 1994.

How to Master Book-Keeping, Peter Marshall (How To Books) 2nd edition 1995

How to Raise Business Finance, Peter Ibbetson (How To Books) 1987

Understanding Your Accounts, A. St. John Price (Kogan Page) 1986

Editing

BAIE Editor's Handbook, (BAIE) 1988

Editing and Design. Book Two: Handling Newspaper Text, Harold Evans (Heinemann) 1974

Editing for Print, Geoffrey Rogers (Macdonald) 1985

Modern Newspaper Editing and Production, F. W. Hodgson, (Heinemann) 1987

Writing

The Complete Guide to Writing Nonfiction, Ed. Glen Evans (Harper and Row) 1988

Editing and Design. Book One: Newsman's English, Harold Evans (Heinemann) 1986

Feature Writing for Newspapers and Magazines, Edward Jay Friedlander and John Lee (Harper and Row) 1988

Handbook of Magazine Article Writing, Ed. Jean Fredette (Writer's Digest Books) 1988

How to Master Business English, Michael Bennie (How To Books) 1991

How to Write a Press Release, Peter Bartram (How To Books) 2nd edition 1995

How to Write a Report, John Bowden (How To Books) 2nd edition 1994

How to Write Business Letters, Ann Dobson (How To Books) 1995

The New Writer, Joan Mitchell (Microsoft Press) 1987

Pocket Style Book (Economist Publications) 1986

The Way to Write Magazine Articles, John Hines (Elm Tree Books) 1987

Writing Feature Articles, Brendan Hennessy (Heinemann) 1989

Design

Creative Newspaper Design, Vic Giles and F. W. Hodgson (Heinemann) 1990

Desktop Publishing Source Book, David Collier and Kay Floyd (Headline) 1989

Design for Magazines, Jan White (R. R. Bowker Company) 1982

Editing and Design. Book Five: Newspaper Design Harold Evans (Heinemann) 1982

Looking Good in Print Roger Parker (Ventana Press) 1988

Newspaper Design Today, Allen Hutt and Bob James (Lund Humphries) 1989

Publication Design, Roy Paul Nelson, published in America by Wm. C. Brown Publishers (ISBN 0-697-08620-8).

Production

Buying Print Cost Effectively, Tony Hart and Peter Kirby (Gower) 1987

The Desktop Publishing Companion, Graham Jones (Sigma Press) 1987

Magazine and Journal Production, Michael Barnard (Blueprint) 1987

The Print Production Handbook, David Bann (Macdonald) 1986

The Print Production Manual (Blueprint) 1988

Marketing and distribution

Business to Business Marketing and Promotion, Martyn Davis (Business Books)

How to Do Your Own Advertising, Michael Bennie (How To Books) 1990

How to Do Your Own PR, Ian Phillipson (How To Books) 1995

How to Market Books, Alison Baverstock (Kogan Page) 1990

How to Publish a Book, Robert Spicer (How To Books) 2nd edition 1995

Successful Marketing for the Small Business, Dave Patten (Kogan Page) 1985

The Writer's Guide to Self Promotion and Publicity, Elane Feldman (Writer's Digest Books) 1990

Legal matters

Essential Law for Journalists, Tom Welsh and Walter Greenwood (Butterworths) 1990

Law and the Media, Tom Crone (Heinemann) 1989

A User's Guide to Copyright, Michael Flint (Butterworths) 1990

Glossary

artwork: the final material from which a newsletter is printed.

assembly: the order in which the printer puts together the material.

back to back: printing on both sides of the paper.

binding: the method in which the newsletter is bound. In most instances this will be by saddle stitching (qv).

bleed: material which is printed across the edge of the paper.

body: the main portion of text.

bromide: artwork produced by typesetting.

bullet: a small black blob used to make a point in a list.

byline: the name of the author.

camera ready: artwork that is produced which can be printed.

casting off: the technique of calculating the amount of space an article will take up in the newsletter.

catchline: the name of an article used as a reference.

Cromalin: a trade name of a method of providing colour proofs.

classifieds: small advertisements.

colour separation: the process of converting colour material into the four process colours used in printing.

contone: a photograph.

crosshead: a single word in the centre of a column used to break up long slabs of text.

copy fitting: the technique of using the cast-off figure to make copy fit in a particular space.

deadline: the date by which a certain task should be completed.

display: a large advertisement, usually with graphics.

DPS: a double-page spread.

drop cap: a large capital letter which extends into the lines of text below it.

dummy: a complete publication prepared as an example.

edition: the copies of a newsletter printed at one time.

editorial: the newsletter's own commentary article.

em: a unit of measurement used by printers. Equivalent to one sixth of an inch.

feature: a long article, not usually of news.

filler: a short item that fills up a tiny piece of space.

film: the material which the printer actually uses to start the printing process. The film is made by photographing the camera ready (qv) artwork.

finishing: printing processes that enhance a newsletter, such as laminating the cover.

flat plan: the basic structure of each edition of the newsletter showing the position of adverts and articles.

folio: the page number.

font: the typeface used and its size.

four-colour: a shorthand for the full colour process printing used to produce high quality publications.

freelance: someone who works on their own account.

galley: a long strip of bromide.

gravure: a high quality printing process.

grid: the basic format for pages of a particular newsletter.

gutter: the space between columns.

hairline: a very thin line.

halftone: a specially prepared photograph which can be printed.

hanging indent: a design feature where the first line of a paragraph extends to the left of the margin.

headline: the main title of each article.

imposition: the method by which the pages are arranged for printing.

imprint: the name and address of the printer.

in pro: re-size a picture in proportion.

ISSN: the International Standard Serial Number.

issue: all the copies of a newsletter produced in one printing.

justification: the method of aligning text in a column so that the left and right edges are vertical.

kerning: the process of moving characters closer together.

keyline: a thin line around the edge of pictures.

layout: the rough design of a page.

leading: the space between lines of text.

letterpress: a form of printing which uses metal characters.

linework: any image which is not a halftone.

litho: the most common method of printing.

mf: more follows; seen at the bottom of each page of text indicating that there is extra material to come.

origination: the production of all the artwork and film.

overlay: a transparent cover over contones (qv) showing the printer what to print and how to print it.

overmatter: extra material that cannot be included.

page proofs: photocopies of each page of artwork.

Pantone: a proprietary system of specifying particular colours.

paste-up: the method of converting galleys (qv) into pages.

pica: a unit of measurement used by printers.

point: a unit of measurement used by printers for specifying type sizes. There are 72 points to one inch.

process colour: the method by which full colour reproduction is achieved by using only four coloured inks.

put to bed: to complete all work on a publication.

registration: the method by which each piece of film is lined up so that accurate printing can take place.

rehash: the re-writing and re-editing of material.

repro: all the planning work involved in colour publications.

Roman: a generic term meaning type that is not bold or italic.

run: the number of copies required.

run on: the number of extra copies needed.

saddle stitch: a staple.

s/s: same size.

scamp: a rough drawing showing a layout.

scanner: a device to input contones and convert them to halftones.

strapline: an explanatory piece of text printed above a headline.

subbing: all of the editorial work involved in preparing material.

subhead: a small headline providing further details.

tint: an area of shade.

transparency: any photographic slide.

trim marks: small marks on the edge of film showing the edge of the page.

u & lc: upper and lower case characters.

unit cost: the price of producing a single copy of a newsletter.

vignette: an area of tint which is graduated.

Web offset: a method of litho printing.

widow: a small item of text left alone at the top of a column.

Index